7/12

Noughts and Crosses

Adapted by Dominic Cooke
from Malorie Blackman's novel

OXFORD
UNIVERSITY PRESS

OXFORD
UNIVERSITY PRESS

Great Clarendon Street, Oxford OX2 6DP

Oxford University Press is a department of the University of Oxford.
It furthers the University's objective of excellence in research,
scholarship, and education by publishing worldwide in

Oxford   New York

Auckland   Cape Town   Dar es Salaam   Hong Kong   Karachi
Kuala Lumpur   Madrid   Melbourne   Mexico City   Nairobi
New Delhi   Shanghai   Taipei   Toronto

With offices in

Argentina   Austria   Brazil   Chile   Czech Republic   France   Greece
Guatemala   Hungary   Italy   Japan   Poland   Portugal   Singapore
South Korea   Switzerland   Thailand   Turkey   Ukraine   Vietnam

British Library Cataloguing in Publication Data

Data available

ISBN 978 0 19 8326946

10 9 8 7 6

Typeset by Palimpsest Book Production Ltd, Grangemouth, Stirlingshire.
Printed and bound by Bell and Bain Ltd., Glasgow.

Acknowledgements

Artwork by Neil Chapman/Beehive Illustration

Elizabeth Eckford quote from *The Long Shadow of Little Rock: A Memoir*
by Daisy Bates (University of Arkansas Press, 2007), copyright © 1986
by Daisy Bates, reprinted by permission of the University of Arkansas
Press, www.uapress.com

Contents

General Introduction

With a fresh, modern look, this classroom-friendly series boasts an exciting range of authors – from Pratchett to Chaucer – whose works have been expertly adapted by such well-known and popular writers as Philip Pullman and David Calcutt. We have also divided the titles available (see page 144) into subcategories – OXFORD *Classic Playscripts* and OXFORD *Modern Playscripts* – to make it even easier for you to think about titles – and periods – you wish to study.

Many teachers use OXFORD *Playscripts* to study the format, style, and structure of playscripts with their students; for speaking and listening assignments; to initiate discussion of relevant issues in class; to meet the Drama objectives of the Framework; as an introduction to the novel of the same title; and to introduce the less able or willing to pre-1914 literature.

At the back of each OXFORD *Playscript*, you will find a brand new Activity section, which not only addresses the points above, but also features close text analysis, and activities that provide support for underachieving readers and act as a springboard for personal writing. Furthermore, the new Activity sections now match precisely the Framework Objectives for Teaching English at Key Stage 3; a chart mapping the Objectives – and the activities that cover them – can be found at the beginning of each Activity section.

Many schools will simply read through the play in class with no staging at all, and the Activity sections have been written with this in mind, with individual activities ranging from debates and designing campaign posters to writing extra scenes or converting parts of the original novels into playscript form.

For those of you, however, who do wish to take to the stage, each OXFORD *Playscript* also features 'A Note on Staging' – a section dedicated to suggesting ways of staging the play, as well as examining the props and sets you may wish to use.

Above all, we hope you will enjoy using OXFORD *Playscripts*, be it on the stage or in the classroom.

What the Adapter Says

When I first read *Noughts and Crosses*, within about twenty pages I knew that this was something that had to be seen on stage. I have always been interested in plays that tackle the crucial question of how we live together. Here was an epic novel that explored big public stories and the effect they have on personal, private experiences. Conveniently, the shape of the novel referred to an existing great play, *Romeo and Juliet*, and the idea of seeing the same event from two different perspectives struck me as being hugely theatrical. It featured two richly drawn and hugely appealing, funny and vulnerable central characters that an audience would immediately connect with. Also, I was aware of how few pieces of theatre are aimed specifically at teenage audiences. This story addresses the painful journey towards adulthood that we all go through; the challenge of breaking away from your parents and going out into the world. Finally, I was attracted to the way in which Malorie Blackman had written the novel in first person narration and dialogue. If the adaptation employed a convention of direct address, I could use Malorie's original words as much as possible.

There were many questions over how to adapt *Noughts and Crosses* for the stage. How would I condense the 450 pages of Malorie Blackman's novel into two hours of theatre? How would the novel's relay race structure work on stage, where it takes longer for an audience to get inside the experience of a character than it does on the page? How would I deal with one of the strokes of genius of the novel, that the reader doesn't discover that the noughts and Crosses are divided on racial lines until a quarter of the way into the story?

I realized early on that this is a novel about the power of human connection to overcome oppression and injustice. The spine of the story is the relationship between Callum and Sephy and the way in which society, represented most crucially by their families, tries to drive them apart. I decided that every scene would either have some effect on or be directly affected by that relationship. This became the guiding principle for how I would shape the stage version. I also determined that I would focus the first half primarily on Callum's story, the second on Sephy's. This would allow the audience to make a deep connection with each of the central characters and give them a surprise when they entered the world of Sephy's family at the start of the second half. In the end I decided that it would impossible to hide the racial divide for the first quarter of the play. In early previews I nodded towards this with a prologue that was performed in shadow. However, in front of an audience this seemed superfluous and we cut it.

It took a long time before the final version took shape. I had several failed attempts, a number of very informative meetings with Malorie, and a very helpful reading with actors of an early draft. With the help of superb advice from Jeanie O'Hare, the Literary Manager at the Royal Shakespeare Company, and sterling support from Malorie herself, I made many changes to the original story. For example, we decided that it would provide more tension in the second half if Sephy was forced to go to boarding school against her will, rather than, as in the novel, choosing to go of her own accord. In some scenes I made characters' problems more explicit and focused them into dramatic choices. In Act 2 Scene 3, Kamal tries to pressure Sephy into participating in a newspaper photo shoot to give a public impression of happy family life. Here we watch her choose between supporting her father's career and being true to herself. With each successive rewrite I changed more and more of Malorie's dialogue to support the very different discipline of telling a story on stage to that of a novel. In some cases I made lines more hidden and subtextual; in others I made them more explicit.

In rehearsals I cut and added whole scenes and reshaped dialogue and story lines. During preview performances in Stratford-upon-Avon, as well as cutting the prologue, I made further changes and clarifications. At the end of the Stratford run, we restaged the show for a UK tour in Newcastle and added a new scene in the hideaway which showed that Callum's feelings for Sephy were still as strong as ever. All through this process Malorie was involved and showed huge generosity and trust in allowing me free rein in making the story work for the stage. I am hugely grateful to her and also the cast of the first production for giving such powerful, moving performances, coming up with many great ideas and bearing with me through the constant chopping and changing.

Dominic Cooke

A Note on Staging

Scenes should flow into one another with no gaps. No blackouts except where stated. There should be a minimum of props and clutter.

Costumes and Props

Act 1

Scene 1	School bags; school books
Scenes 5, 9, 21	TV remote control
Scenes 2, 5, 6, 20	Table and chairs; cutlery and plates
Scene 6	Brown plaster

Act 2

Scenes 1, 13, 22	TV remote control
Scenes 8, 28	Rope and hood
Scenes 3, 5, 9	Wine bottle and wine glass
Scenes 12, 13	Bed or similar
Scenes 14, 21	Envelope; letter-type paper and pen
Scene 21	Newspaper

Cast

Apart from the protagonists and their families, parts should be doubled.

Noughts

Played by white actors

Callum
Meggie
Ryan
Jude
Lynette

Shania
Colin
Leila
Morgan
Pete
Sarah Pike
Kelani Adams
Prisoners

Funeral guests
Shoppers
Execution witnesses

Crosses

Played by black actors

Sephy
Kamal
Jasmine
Minerva

Reporter
Mr Corsa
Joanne
Dionne
Lola
Stanhope
Prison governor
Prison officer
Juno
Mr Pingule
Jack
Clerk
Policemen
Elderly man

Students
Protestors
Shoppers
Execution witnesses
Journalists

ACT ONE

● ●

SCENE 1

The beach.

Sephy   My family's private beach. This was my favourite place in the whole world. Kilometres of coastline that was all ours, with just a couple of signs saying 'private property' and some rickety old wooden fencing at each end, through which Callum and I had made a gap. This was the one place in the world where nobody else would find us. Since Callum's mum stopped working for my mum we'd been meeting here every day. That was three years ago now. And we'd meet here every day forever. No-one could stop us.

Sephy and Callum sit together. The sound of waves.

Callum   Can I kiss you?

Sephy   Pardon?

Callum   Can I kiss you?

Sephy   What on earth for?

Callum   Just to see what it's like.

Sephy   Do you really want to?

Callum   Yeah, I do.

Sephy   Oh, all right then. But make it fast.

Callum faces Sephy. She tilts her head to the left. So does he. She tilts her head to the right. So does he.

Do you want me to tilt my head to the left or the right?

Callum   Er, which side do girls normally tilt their heads when they're being kissed?

9

Sephy	How should I know? Have I ever kissed a boy before?
Callum	Tilt your head to the left then.
Sephy	My left or your left?
Callum	Er… your left
	She does so.
Sephy	Hurry up, before I get a crick in my neck.
	***Callum** licks his lips and moves closer.*
	Oh, no you don't. Wipe your lips first.
Callum	Why?
Sephy	You just licked them.
Callum	Oh. OK.
	***Callum** wipes his lips.*
Sephy	Hurry up.
	***Callum** kisses **Sephy**. After a moment **Sephy** withdraws.*
	Yuk! Callum! What did you do that for?
Callum	It wasn't that bad was it?
Sephy	I don't want your tongue on mine.
Callum	Why not?
Sephy	'Cause… our spit will mix up.
Callum	So? It's meant to.
	***Sephy** considers this.*
Sephy	Let's try it again.
	*They kiss again. After a while **Sephy** pulls away.*
	That's enough.
Callum	Sorry.

Sephy	Why are you apologizing? Didn't you like it?
Callum	It was... OK.
Sephy	Have you ever kissed any girls besides me?
Callum	No.
Sephy	Any nought girls?
Callum	No.
Sephy	Any Cross girls?
Callum	No means no.
Sephy	So why do you want to kiss me?
Callum	We're friends aren't we?
	Pause.
Sephy	What's the matter?
Callum	Nothing.
Sephy	What're you thinking?
	Pause.
Callum	Sephy, do you ever dream of just... escaping? Hopping on the first boat or plane you come across and just getting away from here?
Sephy	This place isn't so bad, is it?
Callum	Depends on your point of view. You're on the inside. With your dad's job and everything. You can't get much more on the inside than the Deputy Prime Minister.
Sephy	If you do go away, will you take me with you?
	Pause. **Callum** *sighs.*
Callum	We'd better get on with it.
	He gets books out of his bag.

Sephy	You've already passed the entrance exam. Why do we still have to do this?
Callum	I don't want to give any of the teachers an excuse to kick me out.
Sephy	You haven't even started school yet and already you're talking about being kicked out. You've got nothing to worry about. You're in now. They accepted you.
Callum	Being in and being accepted are two different things.
Sephy	I've just had a thought. Maybe you'll be in my class. Wouldn't that be great?
Callum	You think so?
Sephy	Wouldn't you like to be in my class?
Callum	It's a bit humiliating for us noughts to be stuck in the baby class.
Sephy	What d'you mean? I'm fourteen.
Callum	I'm nearly sixteen. How would you like to be in a class with kids two years younger than you?
Sephy	The school explained why. You're at least a year behind and –
Callum	Noughts-only schools have no computers, hardly any books. My maths class last year had forty students. How many would you have at Heathcroft?
Sephy	I dunno. Around fifteen.
Callum	Well there you go then. Hardly our fault, is it?
	Pause.
	Sorry. I didn't mean to bite your head off.
Sephy	Are any of your friends from your old school going to join you at Heathcroft?
Callum	No. None of them got in. I wouldn't have either if you hadn't helped me.

12

Pause.

Come on, we'd better get back to work.

Sephy	OK. Maths or history?
Callum	Maths.
Sephy	Yuk.
Callum	It's the universal language.
Sephy	Pardon?
Callum	Look at how many different languages are spoken on our planet. The only thing that doesn't change, no matter what the language, is maths.
	That's probably how we'll talk to aliens from other planets. We'll use maths.
Sephy	Are you winding me up?
	She gets her book out of her bag.

Callum	You should free your mind and think about other cultures and planets and oh, I don't know, just think about the future.
Sephy	I've got plenty of time to think about the future when I'm tons older and don't have much future left, thank you very much.
Callum	There's more to life than just us noughts and you Crosses you know.
Sephy	Don't say that.
Callum	Don't say what?
Sephy	*Us* noughts and *you* Crosses. It makes it sound like... like I'm in one world and you're in another.
Callum	Maybe we are in different worlds.
Sephy	We aren't if we don't want to be.
Callum	If only it was that simple.
Sephy	It is.
Callum	Maybe from where you're sitting.
	Pause.
Sephy	How come I never go to your house anymore? Aren't I welcome?
Callum	Course you are. But the beach is better.
Sephy	Is it because of Lynette? 'Cause if it is, I really don't mind about your sister being...
Callum	Barking?
Sephy	No, not barking, no.
Callum	Then what?
	Pause.
Sephy	Sorry.
Callum	Maybe it'd be better if we don't talk to each other when we're at school.

Sephy	Why on earth not?
Callum	I don't want you to lose any of your friends because of me.
Sephy	But that's just silly. They'll love you.
	Silence.
	What's wrong?
Callum	It's just. It doesn't matter. Give me a hug.
	They go to hug.
Jasmine	*[offstage]* PERSEPHONE! INSIDE! NOW!
Sephy	Cripes! Mother.
Callum	You'd better go.
Sephy	How did she find out I was here?
Callum	Just go.
Sephy	But your lesson…
Jasmine	Persephone! What are you doing?
Callum	Hurry up.
Sephy	See you tomorrow.
	Sephy grabs her things. She quickly kisses Callum on the lips and then runs off.

• •

SCENE 2

	Callum's house.
Callum	Looking at our run down hovel, I could feel the usual burning churning sensation begin to rise up inside me. My stomach tightened, my eyes began to narrow. Soon as I opened the front door, there was our living room with its fifth-hand threadbare nylon carpet and its seventh-hand cloth sofa. Why couldn't my family live in a house like Sephy's?

15

*The **McGregor family** are now seated at the table. **Callum** moves around as he introduces his family.*

My family: *[He goes to his mother]* Three years ago, Mum and Sephy's mother were really close. Mum was nanny to Sephy's sister, and then Sephy. One week, Mrs Hadley and Mum were like best friends and the next week, Mum and I were no longer welcome anywhere near the Hadley house. No idea why. Dad isn't bothered about much – just keeps his head down. Jude, my seventeen year old brother, is a really irritating toad. Ever since I got into Heathcroft, he's become totally unbearable. Lynette, my sister: we've always been close. Closer than Jude and me. But something happened which changed Lynette. An accident. Now she doesn't go out, doesn't talk much, doesn't think much as far as I can tell. She just is 'away with the fairies' as Grandma used to say. I can't get in and she doesn't come out. But her mind takes her to somewhere peaceful, I think. Sometimes I envy her.

The family are halfway through supper.

Meggie	Where've you been, Callum? I was worried sick.

Callum sits.

Well, I'm waiting. Where were you?

Jude	He was with his dagger friend.
Meggie	Don't use that word please, Jude.
Callum	*[Aside]* Jude never called them Crosses. They were always daggers.
Meggie	Well, were you with that girl again?
Callum	No, Mum, I went for a walk. That's all.
Ryan	Meggie, leave the lad alone.
Meggie	That had better be all.

Meggie serves Callum's food.

Callum	Hi Lynny.

Lynette is in her own world.

You alright?

Pause.

Meggie	Where were you walking?
Callum	Oh, round and about.
Meggie	Hmmmm.
Lynette	What am I doing here?

Silence.

I shouldn't be here. I'm not one of you. I'm a Cross.

Jude	What're you talking about? Look at your skin. You're just as white as the rest of us. Whiter.
Lynette	But my skin's a beautiful colour. So dark and rich and wonderful.
Jude	I'm fed up with this. She's a ruddy nutter.
Ryan	Don't talk to your sister like that, please.
Jude	And Callum's no better. Lord of the ruddy manor.
Callum	You don't know what you're talking about.
Ryan	We'd appreciate some peace and quiet at the dinner table, please.
Jude	Look at you peering down your nose at us just because you've come back from your precious dagger girlfriend. You hate us and you hate yourself just because you weren't born one of them. I'm the only one of the three of us who knows what he is and am proud of it.
Callum	Shut up, you brainless –

Jude springs up, ready to hit Callum. Callum matches him.

Jude	Come on then, if you think you're hard enough.
Ryan	I've had a very long day, Jude. Now stop it.

Callum slowly sits down. **Jude** *follows.*

Lynette	I can't be a nought. I just can't.
Meggie	Listen, Lynette.
Lynette	I'm a Cross. Closer to God.
Jude	Stupid cow.
Ryan	Jude!
Lynette	Don't you think I'm beautiful, Callum?
Callum	Yes, I do Lynette. Very.

Pause.

Ryan	Ready for school tomorrow, Callum?
Callum	Ready as I'll ever be.
Meggie	I hope you're not making a mistake.
Ryan	He's not.
Jude	He doesn't need to go to their schools. We don't have to mix with them.
Callum	What's wrong with mixing?
Meggie	It never works. We should be able to educate our own. Not wait for the Crosses to do it for us.
Ryan	You never used to believe that.
Meggie	Well I'm not as naïve as I used to be. Jasmine Hadley opened my eyes.
Callum	*[Aside]* What would satisfy all the noughts and Crosses who felt the same as Mum? Separate countries? Separate planets? How far away is far enough?
Ryan	Meggie, if our boy is going to get anywhere in this life, he has learn to play the game. He has just got to be better at it than them. That's all.
Meggie	That's all!

Ryan	Don't you want something more for your son than we had?
Meggie	How can you ask me that?
Callum	I'm sure everything will be fine, Mum.
Jude	You'll soon think you're too good for us.
Ryan	Of course he won't. You'll be on your best behaviour, won't you? You'll be representing all of us noughts at the school.
Callum	Why do I have to represent all noughts? Why can't I just represent myself?
Ryan	You must show them they're wrong about us. Show them we're just as good as they are.
Meggie	He doesn't need to go to their stuck-up school to show them that.
Jude	He'll soon be as bad as they are.
Ryan	A son of mine at Heathcroft School. Imagine that!

● ●

SCENE 3

At the school gates.

Sephy	First day of school. I groaned at the thought. At least today would be different from the start of every other new term. Three noughts, including Callum, were starting at my school. I wanted to show him the playing fields and the swimming pool, the gym and music rooms, the dining hall and science labs. And I'd introduce him to all my friends. It was going to be wonderful. But as I approached the corner, shouting like an angry wave, they rolled towards me.

An angry Cross crowd – parents and students.

Crowd	No blankers in our school! No blankers in our school! No blankers in our school!

Mr Corsa	As the Headmaster of this school it is my legal duty to ask you that you let the new students enter the school.

The crowd continues.

Crowd	No blankers in our school! No blankers in our school! No blankers in our school!

*Sephy watches as **Callum, Colin** and **Shania,** all noughts, try to push their way through the crowd to get to the school entrance. **Police** try to push the crowd into two separate groups. **Mr Corsa** is in the other side of the crowd looking on. **Shania** is hit by a stone.*

Protestor 1	One of them is hurt.
Protestor 2	A blanker's hurt.

*Other protestors cheer. The struggle continues. **Sephy** gets through.*

Sephy	Mr Corsa, we have to help that girl. She's hurt!

He doesn't move.

Sephy addresses the crowd.

Stop it! Just stop it!

Crowd	Blankers out! Blankers out!
Sephy	Stop it! You're all behaving like animals!

The crowd silences.

Worse than animals! Like blankers!

*As **Callum** and **Sephy** turn to us to speak, the crowd melts away leaving them on their own.*

Callum	*[Aside]* She didn't say that. She couldn't have. Not Sephy… I'm not a blanker. I may be a nought but I'm worth more than nothing. I'm not a blanker. A waste of time and space. A zero. A nothing.

SCENE 4

	At the beach.
Sephy	Callum, don't look at me like that.
	Pause.
	What would you like me to say?
	Pause.
	I said I'm sorry.
Callum	I know.
Sephy	It's just a word.
Callum	Just a word…
Sephy	Sticks and stones, Callum. It's one word, that's all.
Callum	If you'd slapped me or kicked me or punched me or even stabbed me it would've stopped hurting sooner or later. But I'll never forget what you called me, Sephy. Never. Not if I live to be five hundred.
Sephy	I didn't mean it . I didn't mean you. I was trying to help.
Callum	Sephy…
Sephy	Please, I'm so sorry.
Callum	Maybe we shouldn't see so much of each other any more.
Sephy	Callum, no. I said I was sorry.
	Pause.
Callum	Promise me something.
Sephy	Anything.
Callum	Promise me that you'll never ever use that word again.
Sephy	I promise.

[Aside] I'd never fully realized just how powerful words could be. Whoever came up with that 'sticks and stones may break my bones' rubbish was talking out of their armpit. Why did I say that word? It was as if I was outside myself. More and more I was beginning to feel like a spectator in my own life. I had to make a choice. I had to decide what kind of friend Callum was going to be to me.

• •

SCENE 5

***Callum's** house. At the dinner table.*

Ryan	Are you OK, son? I went down to Heathcroft as soon as I heard what was going on, but the police wouldn't let me in.
Callum	Why not?
Ryan	I had 'no official business on the premises' – unquote.

Pause.

So how was school? How were your lessons, son?

Callum	It was fine, Dad.

[Aside] Except that the teachers totally ignored us, and the Crosses used any excuse to bump into us and knock our books on the floor, and even the dinner ladies made sure they served everyone else in the queue before us.

Jude	You were on the telly. So was your little friend. The whole world heard what she said.
Callum	She didn't mean it like that.
Jude	She didn't mean it? That's what she told you, was it? How can you not mean to say something like that?
Meggie	I see Miss Sephy is turning out to be just like her mother.
Ryan	You're better off without that job.
Meggie	You don't have to tell me twice. I admit I miss the money but I wouldn't go back for all the stars in space. Anyone who can

put up with that stuck-up cow Mrs Hadley is a saint as far as I'm concerned.

Callum   You were friends once.

Meggie   Friends? We were never friends. She patronized me and I put up with it 'cause I needed a job – that's all.

Callum   *[Aside]* That wasn't how I remembered it.

Ryan clicks the remote control.

Ryan   Shush, everyone. The news is on.

*The **news reporter**, a Cross, enters the McGregors' kitchen, perhaps sitting at the table. When reading the news, the reporter speaks directly to the other characters on stage. This convention is used whenever the TV is watched. There is no TV set or video screen on stage.*

Reporter   *[To the family]* Today Kamal Hadley, Deputy Prime Minister, declared that there would be no hiding place, no safe haven for those noughts misguided enough to join the Liberation Militia.

[To offstage] Is it true, Mr Hadley, that your government's decision to allow selected noughts in our schools was a direct result of pressure from the Liberation Militia?

*Kamal enters the kitchen. The **reporter** turns to him.*

Kamal   Not at all. This government does not allow itself to be whitemailed by illegal terrorist groups. We acted on a Pangean Economic Community directive that the government had been on the verge of implementing anyway. Our decision to allow the crème-de-la-crème of nought youth to join our educational institutions makes sound social and economic sense.

Callum   *[Aside]* Pompous twit!

Kamal   The Liberation Militia are misguided terrorists and we will leave no stone unturned in our efforts to bring them to justice.

Jude   Long live the Liberation Militia!

Ryan	Too right, son.
Meggie	Shhh.

Jude and Ryan look at each other.

Reporter	There have been unconfirmed reports that the car bomb found outside the International Trade Centre last month was the work of the Liberation Militia. What attempts are being made to find those responsible?
Kamal	Our highest priority is to bring them to justice. Political terrorism which results in the death or serious injury of even one Cross always has been and always will be a capital crime. Those found guilty will suffer the death sentence...

*Sephy enters with her own remote, which she clicks. **The reporter** and **Kamal** leave the stage.*

Sephy	Politics, politics, politics. I've grown up with it rammed down my throat. I'm not interested in being caught up with it in any manner, shape or form, whether Dad is on the telly or not.

● ●

SCENE 6

In the school dining hall. The school bell rings.

Callum	I lined up in the food queue. I collected my chicken and mushroom pie with boiled-to-death trimmings, my jam tart with custard and my carton of milk and, taking a deep breath I headed for the table where the other noughts were sitting.

*Sephy approaches the noughts' table. **Shania** wears a large brown plaster on her face.*

Sephy	Do you mind if I join you?

She sits at the table.

Callum	What do you think you're doing?
Sephy	Sitting down.
Callum	Go away, Sephy.

Sephy	Why should I? I want to sit here.

Callum moves to another seat. Sephy smiles at the other noughts who have been staring at her. They instantly look away. She offers Shania her hand.

Hi. I'm Sephy Hadley. Welcome to Heathcroft.

Shania wipes her hand clean on her tunic. She then takes Sephy's hand and shakes it slowly.

Shania	I'm Shania.
Sephy	That's a pretty name. What does it mean?
Shania	It doesn't mean anything.
Sephy	My mother told me my name means 'serene night'. But Callum will tell you I'm anything but serene.

Shania smiles tentatively.

How's your cut?

Shania	It's OK. It'll take more than a stone to dent my head.
Sephy	The plaster's a bit noticeable.
Shania	They don't sell pink plasters. Only dark brown ones.
Sephy	Oh. I suppose they do.

Mr Corsa approaches.

Mr Corsa	Sephy, just what do you think you're doing?
Sephy	Pardon?
Mr Corsa	What're you doing?
Sephy	I'm eating my lunch.
Mr Corsa	Don't be facetious.
Sephy	I'm not. I'm eating my lunch.
Mr Corsa	Get back to your own table – at once.

Everyone in the food hall watches, engrossed.

Sephy	But I want to sit here.
Mr Corsa	Get back to your own table – NOW!
Sephy	I'm sitting with my friend Callum.

Mr Corsa grabs Sephy's arm and pulls her out of the chair.

Mr Corsa	Persephone Hadley, you will come with me.

As Sephy is dragged away she looks at Callum. He looks away.

Shania	Serves her right. Coming over to our table and acting the big 'I am'.
Callum	She didn't. It wasn't like that.
Shania	Of course it was. She wanted to lord it over us. A little kid like that sitting at our table.
Callum	What're you talking about?
Shania	Just because her dad's in the government, that Sephy Hadley thought she'd play Lady Magnanimous and sit with us. I bet she'll go and scrub her hand now I shook it.

The food hall melts away, leaving Callum.

Callum	I walked out of the food hall and out of the building and out of the school, my steps growing ever faster and more frantic –

until by the time I was out of the school I was running. Running until my back ached and my feet hurt and my heart was ready to burst and still I kept running. I ran all the way out of the town and down to the beach.

Callum collapses on the sand and punches his bag over and over.

Sephy! Sephy! Sephy!

Sephy approaches. She stares at Callum, full of anger.

Sephy	Turning your back on me like that. Some best friend.
Callum	Alright, alright.

Pause.

Sephy	You're a snob, Callum. And I never realized it until now. I thought you were better than that. Above all that nonsense. But you're just like all the others. 'Crosses and noughts shouldn't be friends. Crosses and noughts shouldn't even live on the same planet together.'
Callum	That's rubbish. I don't believe any of that, you know I don't.
Sephy	Well if you're not a snob, you're a hypocrite, which is even worse. I'm OK to talk to as long as no-one can see us. As long as no-one knows.
Callum	Don't talk to me like that.
Sephy	Which one is it Callum? Are you a snob or a hypocrite?
Callum	Get lost, Sephy.
Sephy	With pleasure.

Sephy goes to leave.

Callum	I'm sorry.
Sephy	I thought that was my job in this friendship. Saying sorry. Sorry for being at a good school. Sorry for saying the wrong thing. Sorry for sitting at your table. I'm sick of feeling guilty all the time. It's not my fault that things are the way they are.

Callum	I know.
Sephy	Then stop blaming me. And if you can't, then leave me alone.
	She exits.
Callum	Why had my life suddenly become so complicated? For the last year all I could ever think about was going to school. Sephy's school. I was so busy concentrating on getting into Heathcroft that I didn't give any thought to what it'd be like when I actually got there.

• •

SCENE 7 / ACT 1 marginalia

SCENE 7

The girls' toilets. **Sephy** *is in a cubicle.*

Sephy	There is a proverb which says, 'Be careful what you wish for, because you might just end up getting it!'. I never really knew what that meant until now. All those months helping Callum with his work so he'd pass the Heathcroft entrance exam and we could go to the same school together, be in the same class together even. And now it had all come true. And it was horrible. Everything was going wrong. Well… I couldn't hide in here forever. And who was I hiding from anyway? Well, all those people who'd been pointing and whispering as I walked past them in the school corridor for starters – but mainly from Callum. I was afraid to face him. If I didn't see him, I could pretend nothing between us had changed.

The school bell rings.

OK! Here goes.

Sephy opens the cubicle door. Three Cross girls, **Lola, Joanne** *and* **Dionne** *confront* **Sephy**.

Lola	We want to have a word with you.
Sephy	And it has to be in here, does it, Lola?

Joanne shoves Sephy.

Joanne	About what you did yesterday.

Sephy	What's it to you?
	Lola slaps Sephy.
Lola	I don't care if your dad's God Almighty himself. Stick to your own kind. If you sit with the blankers again, everyone in this school will treat you like one of them.
Joanne	You need to wake up and check which side you're on.
Dionne	What d'you want to be around them for anyway? They smell funny and they eat weird food and everyone knows that none of them are exactly close friends with soap and water.
	The three girls laugh.
Sephy	What a load of rubbish. Callum has a wash every day and he doesn't smell. None of them do.
	Lola, Joanne and Dionne look at each other. Lola pushes Sephy down on the toilet. Sephy tries to stand. Lola pushes her down again.
Lola	We're only going to say this once. Choose your friends very carefully. If you don't stay away from those blankers, you'll find you don't have a single friend left in this school.
Sephy	I bet none of you has even spoken to a nought before.
Joanne	Of course we have. When they serve us in shops and restaurants…
Dionne	In burger bars!
	They laugh.
Joanne	Besides we don't need to speak to them. We see them on the news practically every other day. Everyone knows they're all muggers and they hang around in gangs and knife people and listen to crap music.
Lola	Look at the facts. It's on the news. The news doesn't lie.
Sephy	The news lies all the time. They tell us what they think we want to hear. The majority of noughts are decent, hardworking people.

Joanne	Who told you that? Your dad?
Lola	I bet it was one of her blanker friends. Blank by name and blank by nature.
Sephy	What are you talking about?
Lola	Blank, white faces with not a hint of colour in them. Blank minds which can't hold a single, original thought. Blank, blank, blank.
Sephy	You ought to sell that horse manure worldwide. You'd make a fortune. Noughts are people, just like us. You're the ones who are stupid and ignorant and…

Lola slaps Sephy. Sephy punches Lola in the stomach. She continues hitting Lola. Lola and Joanne grab one of Sephy's arms.

| Dionne | Blanker lover. You've had this coming for a long time. |

Dionne beats up Sephy.

• •

SCENE 8

Outside Sephy's house.

| Callum | When Shania told me the news about Sephy, my feet scarcely touched the ground. I didn't stop until I was standing in front of the Hadleys' iron gates. |

Callum, on one side of the stage, presses the entryphone for a long time. Sarah Pike appears. (No real phones used.)

Sarah	Yes?
Callum	Sephy?
Sarah	This is Mrs Hadley's secretary.
Callum	Sarah, it's Callum McGregor. I want to see Sephy – please.
Sarah	I'm afraid the doctor says she's not to be disturbed.

The sound of the receiver being replaced. Sarah exits. Callum puts his finger on the buzzer and holds it there. Sarah re-enters.

Yes?

He stops buzzing.

Callum	I want to see Sephy. Is she all right?
Sarah	She's badly bruised and very upset. The doctor has advised that she be kept at home for the rest of the week.
Callum	What happened? Why?
Jasmine	*[Offstage]* Who is it, Sarah?
Sarah	It's all under control, Mrs Hadley.
Jasmine	Is it that McGregor boy?
Sarah	Yes, Mrs Hadley.

*Enter **Jasmine**. She takes the receiver from **Sarah**.*

Jasmine	This is Persephone's mother, can I help you?
Callum	I'd like to see Sephy, please.
Jasmine	I believe my daughter was attacked by three girls for sitting at your lunch table yesterday. As I understand it, you turned your back on her and told her to go away. Is that right?
Callum	I was trying to protect her. I didn't want her to get bullied for being my friend.
Jasmine	Hmmm. Likely story.

***Jasmine** hands the receiver back to **Sarah**.*

Sarah, make sure this boy doesn't set foot here again.

Callum	Please let me see Sephy.
Sarah	You're going to have to go now.
Callum	Please…
Sarah	I'm sorry.

Sarah exits.

SCENE 9

Sephy's bedroom.

Sephy   There was absolutely nothing on the telly. With a sigh I plumped for the news. I looked at the screen without really watching it. The newsreader was finishing the story of a stockbroker who'd been sent to prison for fraud. He was now talking about three nought robbers who'd smashed in the front of an exclusive jewellery store and made off on motorbikes with gems and jewellery and watches worth close to a million. Why was it that when noughts committed criminal acts, the fact that they were noughts was always pointed out? The stockbroker was a Cross. The newsreader didn't even mention it.

She flicks off the TV with the remote.

I closed my eyes. I tried to find something to focus on besides the bruises over my body. Callum… Even thinking about him wasn't bringing me the comfort it usually did. My best friend had turned his back on me. Not a word since Lola and the others laid into me. Ruddy noughts. This was all their fault. If it hadn't been for them… And as for Lola and her stooges. I was going to get them, if it was the very last thing I did. I was going to get them – and good. I opened my eyes and stared out into nothing but hate.

SCENE 10

*Callum's house – evening. **Lynette** and **Jude** are squaring up to each other.*

Lynette   You're a git, Jude, and a vulgar git at that!

Jude   At least I'm not living a lie.

Lynette   And what's that supposed to mean?

Jude   You're white. Face it.

Callum	Leave her alone Jude, you bully.
	Jude hits Lynette. She hits him back. They start fighting and Ryan comes between them.
Jude	Look at you! You think you're too damn good to breathe the same air as us. Well I've got news for you. When the daggers look at you, they see someone who's just as white as me.
Lynette	I'm not like you. I'm different.
	Jude pushes past Ryan.
Ryan	Stop it, Jude.
	Jude grabs Lynette and takes her to a mirror. He forces her to look at their reflection.
Jude	See! You're the same as me. As white as me. I'm sick and tired of you looking down your nose at me. If you hate what you are, do something about it. Just die or something! And if there is a God, you'll come back as one of those ruddy daggers you love so much, and then I can stop feeling guilty about hating you.
	Lynette falls to the floor.
Callum	Do something, Dad.
Ryan	Jude, that's enough. More than enough.
Jude	It's time she heard the truth from someone. Who else is going to say it?
Callum	You're always so sure you're right, aren't you? You make me sick. Lynette isn't the only one here who can't stand you.
Jude	She's just a waste of space.
Ryan	*[To Jude]* What the hell is wrong with you? She's your sister, for goodness' sake.
Jude	Oh get lost, Dad.
	Ryan spins Jude around and slaps his face.

Ryan	Don't you ever, ever talk to me like that. I'm too old and have had to contend with too much crap in my life to put up with disrespect in my own house. You have no idea what your sister's been through, so how dare you judge her?
Jude	Yeah, yeah, yeah, we all know, she had an accident. Poor little Lynny. That was two years ago. Isn't it time she got over it?
Ryan	You don't know the first thing about what your sister's been through.
Callum	It wasn't an accident was it?

Pause.

Ryan	Lynny and her boyfriend were attacked. By our own. Three or four nought men beat Lynette's lad nearly to death. And she was so badly hurt she had to spend two weeks in hospital.
Callum	I knew it. I knew she wasn't staying with Aunt Charlotte.
Jude	Why didn't she want us to know?
Ryan	Because her boyfriend was a Cross.
Jude	I might have guessed.
Ryan	She was so ashamed she begged us not to tell you.
Jude	Maybe that will teach her to stick to her own kind.
Ryan	Your sister was put into intensive care by those animals. They left her for dead. Is it any wonder that she can't bear to think of herself as one of us any more? Now leave her alone. Or you'll have me to answer to. D'you hear me? Jude, do you hear me?

Pause.

Jude	Yes, Dad.
Lynette	Where's Jed, Daddy?
Ryan	Honey, Jed went away a long, long time ago. Let me get you up.

Lynette	Where am I?
Ryan	At home. You're safe now. I'm here.
Callum	We'll look after you, Lynny.
Lynette	Where's Jed?
Ryan	Listen, sweetheart, Jed and his family moved away a long time ago. He's gone.
Lynette	Not a long time ago. Yesterday. Last week.
Ryan	It was years ago.
Lynette	It's my eighteenth birthday next week.
Ryan	No, love, you're twenty. Twenty last April. Come on, let's get up.
Lynette	I thought I was seventeen. Eighteen. I don't know what I thought.
Ryan	Lynette, please –

*Jude reaches out his hand to **Lynette**.*

Jude	I'm sorry, Lynny.

*She takes **Jude's** hand and puts it next to hers. She looks at them closely.*

Lynette	Your hands are the same as mine. The same as theirs.

Lynette goes to exit.

Callum	I'll come with you.
Lynette	No, I'll be alright.

*Lynette exits. **Jude** and **Ryan** look at each other.*

Callum	I caught sight of the three of us in the mirror. My face was the reflection of Dad and Jude. My expression was theirs. My thoughts and feelings and hates and fears were all theirs, just as theirs were mine, and though I like to think I'm quick and on the ball. I hadn't even realized. Until now.

SCENE 11

In the classroom. History lesson.

Sephy   Jeez! Time crawled like it was dragging a blue whale behind it. That sounded like something Callum would say... Something Callum would've said – when he used to talk to me. When he used to be my friend. The teacher was blathering on about simultaneous equations like they were the best thing since computers were invented. And every word was flying zip-zap straight over my head. When was the bell going to sound? Come on... come on...

The bell sounds.

At last!

Sephy gathers her books up and makes to leave.

Callum   Sephy, wait.

Sephy sits.

Callum   How are you? Are you OK now?

Sephy   Yes, thank you.

Callum   I'm glad.

Sephy   Are you? You could have fooled me.

Callum   What does that mean?

Other students are listening.

Sephy   Don't pretend you were worried about me. You didn't come and see me once. You didn't even send me a card.

Callum   I came to see you every day. Every single day. Your mum gave orders that I wasn't to be let in. I stood outside your gates every afternoon after school. Ask your mum... no, ask Sarah Pike if you don't believe me.

Pause.

	Wild horses couldn't have kept me away.
Sephy	I have to go now.
Callum	Look, meet me in our special place after dinner tonight. We can't talk here.
	Sephy turns to walk away.
	If you're not there, I'll understand.
Sephy	Goodbye, Callum.

● ●

SCENE 12

In Callum's bedroom.

Callum	Since Lynny and Jude's fight, neither of them had spoken to each other. Not a word. That evening, as I was finishing my homework, there was a knock at my bedroom door…
Lynette	It's me. Can I come in?
Callum	Course.
	Lynette comes in.
	You OK?
Lynette	No. You?
Callum	I'll survive.
Lynette	How's school?
Callum	Well, I'm learning a lot.
Lynette	Tough going, huh?
Callum	Nightmare.
Lynette	Reckon you'll stick with it?
Callum	I'm in now. I'm not about to let them push me out.
Lynette	How do you do it, Callum?

Callum	Do what?
Lynette	Keep going.

Pause.

Callum	I suppose because I know what I want.
Lynette	Which is?

Pause.

Callum	To be someone. To make a difference, I guess.
Lynette	Which means more to you? Being someone or making a difference?

***Callum** laughs.*

What's so funny?

Callum	Nothing. It's just that you and me talking like this, it reminds me of the old days.
Lynette	You haven't answered my question, and don't try to wriggle out of it! Which means more – being someone or making a difference?
Callum	I don't know. Being someone, I guess. Having a large house and money in the bank and not needing to work and being respected wherever I go. When I'm educated and I've got my own business there won't be a single person in the world who'll be able to look down on me – nought or Cross.
Lynette	Being someone, eh? I would've put money on you choosing the other one!
Callum	What's the point in making a difference if you've got nothing to show for it personally, if there's not even any money in it?

Pause.

Are you disappointed in me?

Lynette	You've always been so focused. You've always known exactly where you wanted to end up. I hope it works out for you.

Pause.

You know what I miss? I miss being bonkers!

Callum	Don't say that.

Lynette	I do. I know I was living in a fantasy world before, but at least I was somewhere. Now I'm nowhere.

Callum	That's not true.

Lynette	Isn't it?

Pause.

Callum	Lynny, d'you remember my seventh birthday? You took me to see my first film at the cinema. There was just you and me in the whole place and you got annoyed because I wouldn't take my eyes off the screen. Not for a second.

Lynette	I told you you were allowed to blink. D'you remember? That the screen wasn't going to disappear.

Pause.

Callum	Lynny, you are alright aren't you?

Lynette	I don't know.

Callum	Things will get better.

Lynette	I want to believe that. I really do.

Callum	I'm at Heathcroft High aren't I? A few years ago that would have been impossible. Unthinkable.

Lynette	But none of their universities will take you.

Callum	You don't know that. By the time I'm ready to leave school they might.

Lynette	And then what?

Callum	I'll get a good job. And I'll be on my way up.

Lynette	Doing what?

Callum	You sound just like Jude.

Lynette goes to leave.

Sorry. That was below the belt.

She stops.

It's not too late for you to go to college.

Lynette   How would we pay for that? Anyway I'm not like you. I don't have what it takes.

Callum   Of course you do. You've never given yourself the chance.

Lynette   Just remember, when you're floating up and up in your bubble, that bubbles burst. The higher you climb, the further you have to fall.

She exits.

SCENE 13

The beach.

Callum   Persephone, you have to believe me. I did come to visit you, I swear.

Pause.

Sephy   I believe you.

Callum   You spoke to Sarah.

Sephy   Didn't have to.

Callum   I don't understand.

Sephy   I just believe you. Besides, it sounds like the sort of thing my mother would do.

Pause.

It'll be winter soon. It'll be harder for me to come and meet you here. Mother won't allow it.

Callum   Who beat you up?

Sephy	What does it matter?
Callum	You don't want them to get away with it, do you?
Sephy	There's not a lot I can do about it now. I was going to tell Corsa and get them expelled or put drawing-pins in their shoes or whatever but they're not worth it. I don't want to waste any more energy on them. It happened and now it's over, and I just want to forget about it.
Callum	I was just curious. Besides, what could I do? I'm just a lowly nought. Not on their level. Or yours.
Sephy	Stop it.
Callum	Stop what?
Sephy	Callum, it's me. Sephy. I'm not your enemy.
Callum	I never said…

Sephy takes Callum's face in her hands.

Sephy	Look at me, Callum.

He is tense. Resisting. Then he starts to relax.

I'm your friend and I always will be.

Callum	Sorry.

They hug. Sephy lets go of him.

• •

SCENE 14

At Callum's house.

Callum	*[Aside]* When I got home, Lynette was missing.
Meggie	Jude and Lynette fighting? Ryan, I can't believe you stood by and let it happen. I go to visit my sister for one evening and the whole family falls apart. Why didn't you tell me what had happened? You are the most ineffectual, useless man it's ever been my misfortune to come across.

Jude	It's not Dad's fault, Mum.
Meggie	And you can shut right up. I'm sick to the back teeth of this belief you have, that you and your opinions are always right. You've been picking on your sister and goading her for months now.
Jude	Well you've been picking on me, so that makes us about even.
Meggie	I've been picking on you – as you call it – because you're not doing anything with your life. You could work with your dad in the lumberyard or do an apprenticeship with Old Man Tony but…
Jude	Old Man Tony is always bombed off his trolley! Light a match in front of his mouth and the whole street would go up in flames. And I don't want to get stuck in his ruddy bakery.
Meggie	It's an honest job.
Jude	I don't want an honest job.
Meggie	You don't know what you want.
Jude	Yes, I do. I want to go back to school.
Callum	[Aside] Since when did Jude want to go back to school?
Meggie	Jude, we've been through this before. We didn't have the money to keep you in school. I lost my job, remember? Aren't you going to stand up for me, Ryan? Will you always be such an ineffectual, useless…
Jude	But you found the money for Callum to go.

The doorbell rings. **Ryan** *goes offstage to answer it.*

Policeman	[Offstage] Mr McGregor?
Ryan	[Offstage] Yes?
Policeman	[Offstage] May we come in?
Ryan	[Offstage] Please.

Two **Cross policemen** *enter with* **Ryan.** **Lynette** *walks behind them.*

Policeman	I'm Sergeant Collins and this is Constable Jones.
Ryan	Officers?
Collins	You have a daughter called Lynette?
Meggie	What's happened?
Collins	I'm very sorry, sir, ma'am. I'm afraid I've got some bad news.

They all freeze behind **Callum.** **Lynette** *watches.*

Callum   When the police told us the news, Lynette entered my head and filled my thoughts and spun around me and danced through me until it felt like she was swallowing me up. Mum let out a howl like a wounded animal and sank to her knees. Jude took a step forward and then stopped. The two police officers looked away. The seconds ticked past. Dad hugged Mum, rocking her. Mum didn't speak and she didn't cry. She didn't make a sound.

The family leave the room. **Lynette** *stays.*

For the first time in my life I hated my sister. Hated her guts. She'd given in. She'd given up on life and left me to live it for the both of us. From that moment, I swore that nothing would ever make me do the same as her. Nothing.

SCENE 15

	At Callum's house. Lynette's wake.
Sephy	It'd only been three years since Callum's mum had worked for mine. Three short years. But walking into his house was like walking into a room full of strangers.
	*The room is filled with only nought guests huddled in groups. **Jude** is tipsy. **Meggie** and **Ryan** are close together. **Sephy** approaches **Meggie** and **Ryan**. The room goes quiet.*
	Mr McGregor, Mrs McGregor, I just wanted to tell you how sorry I am about Lynette. I hope I'm not intruding or anything.
Meggie	You're not intruding, Persephone. Thank you for coming. Can I get you a drink?
	***Sephy** looks around at the hostile faces staring at her.*
Sephy	No, I don't think I should stay.
Meggie	Nonsense. You've come this far, you can't leave without a drink. Can she, Ryan?
	Pause.
	Ryan?
	***Ryan** doesn't respond.*
Sephy	I'll go.
Callum	Sephy…
Jude	Who told you to come here in the first place? You and your false sympathy aren't wanted.
Meggie	Jude, that's enough.
Jude	If she cares so much, where was she for the last three years when Lynette was out of her head and we didn't have two beans to rub together to get Lynny the help she needed?

Where was this dagger when you got fired, Mum, and I had to drop out of school?

Jude gives Sephy a shove. Some of the guests gasp.

And then you have the gall to come over here –

Sephy	Mrs McGregor, Mr McGregor –
Ryan	Just go, Miss Hadley.
Sephy	But I haven't done anything –
Ryan	That's right, you haven't. You come in here with your designer dress which cost more than I make in a year and we're supposed to be grateful. Is that how it works?
Sephy	No…
Jude	Just go away. Go on, get out, before I do something I'll regret.

Callum guides Sephy's arm.

Callum	Sephy, I'll –
Ryan	Let her go. Noughts and Crosses don't mix, son.

Sephy rushes out. The crowd resumes talking.

Meggie	*[To Jude]* You had no right to do that.
Ryan	Oh, yes he did. She wasn't wanted here. Jude told her the truth.
Jude	Good on you, Dad.
Meggie	The girl wasn't doing any harm, Ryan. She only came here out of sympathy.
Ryan	Out of guilt, more like.
Meggie	She was paying her respects.
Ryan	She and her kind can go to hell. I don't want those daggers anywhere near me.
Meggie	Ryan!

Ryan	I've had enough, Meggie. I've had enough. My ineffectual days are over.
Callum	*[Aside]* I thought Dad's motto was to live and let live. When did that change? When Lynny died? Or maybe it was there all the time and I'd just chosen not to see it.

• •

SCENE 16

The beach. **Callum** *and* **Sephy** *sit as before.*

Sephy	I didn't mean any harm, Callum.
Callum	Well *I* know that, but…
Sephy	But it wasn't the best idea I've ever had in my life.
Callum	You've had better.
Sephy	I can't seem to do anything right at the moment.
	Pause.
	I am sorry about your sister, Callum. I just wanted to show how much… I thought sending a card would be a bit…
Callum	Impersonal?
Sephy	Exactly. It was just a spur of the moment thing to walk over to your house. I thought it might be a comfort to you, knowing I was there.
	Pause.
	I am there for you, you know.
Callum	I know.
	Pause.
Sephy	This is growing up I guess, isn't it?
Callum	I think it is.
Sephy	Would you put your arm around me, please?

Pause.

If you'd rather not.

Callum No, it's not that.

Pause.

It's just… Never mind.

Callum *puts his arm around* **Sephy.** *She puts her head on his shoulder. They watch the sea.*

● ●

Callum's *living room.*

Callum Lynette's funeral was over three months ago now and Dad wasn't the only one who'd changed. Most nights Mum had taken to going for walks, returning long after I'd gone to bed and was meant to be asleep. Crossmas had come and gone without much cheer. The new year had started and here we all were, occupying opposite points on the compass. And on top of that, Jude and Dad were doing something where I wasn't wanted…

Jude *and* **Ryan** *study a map in silence.* **Meggie** *puts her coat on.* **Callum** *watches.*

Meggie I'm going out.

Ryan Where?

Meggie For a walk.

Ryan Meggie, how much longer are you going to carry on like this?

Meggie Like what?

Ryan Why won't you talk to me?

Meggie Will you give that up?

Ryan No.

Meggie	Then we have nothing to say to each other.
	Meggie leaves the room in disgust.
Ryan	Meggie…
	The door slams behind her.
Callum	What's going on, Dad?
Ryan	Come on, Jude, we've got work to do.
Callum	Where're you going?
Ryan	Out.
Callum	Out where?
Ryan	To a meeting.
Jude	Dad.
Callum	What meeting?
Ryan	None of your business.
Callum	Where is it?
Jude	That's none of your business either.
Callum	How come Jude gets to go with you and I don't?
Ryan	Because you're not old enough.
Callum	Please let me come with you.
Jude	No way.
Callum	I won't be any trouble.
Jude	Yeah, right!
	Pause.
Ryan	Callum, you're not coming with us.
Callum	Why not? If Jude's old enough to join the Liberation Militia then so am I.
	Pause.

Ryan	I don't know what Jude's been telling you, son, but you shouldn't believe everything you hear.
Callum	I worked it out for myself. I'm not stupid. Besides, you haven't exactly been brilliant at hiding it.

Pause.

Jude	I didn't say anything, Dad, I swear.
Ryan	Callum, you must promise me never to mention this to anyone.
Callum	OK.
Ryan	OK isn't good enough. This could cost us our lives.
Callum	I swear I won't tell anyone.
Jude	You'd better not. Especially your dagger friend.

Pause.

Callum	So can I come with you now?
Ryan	We're going to a meeting and you're way too young. Besides, if you were seen it'd be the end of your school career. Is that what you want?
Callum	I don't care. I'm just wasting my time at Heathcroft and everyone knows it. Colin's dropped out and Shania's been expelled for no reason and everyone's taking bets on how long I'm going to last. Besides I was thinking of leaving anyway.
Ryan	Over my dead body. You are going to school and you'll stay at school until you're eighteen and then you'll go on to university. Do I make myself clear?

Pause.

Callum, I asked you a question. You will not leave school without any qualifications. Understand?

Callum	Yeah, OK, OK.

Jude and Ryan go out.

SCENE 18

The classroom.

Sephy   I started watching people – noughts and Crosses. Their faces, their body language, the way they spoke to their own kind. The way they spoke to others. And there were so many differences, they swamped the similarities. Noughts relaxed around each other in a way they rarely did around Crosses. And Crosses were constantly on their guard when near noughts. Bags got clutched tighter, footsteps quickened, voices grew bigger and brusquer. All our lives criss-crossing but never really touching. A world full of strangers living with all that fear. Nothing was a given any more. Not my life. Not theirs. Nothing.

SCENE 19

Callum's house.

Callum   Saturday. Eighteen days and five months after Lynette's death. My sixteenth birthday in February had come and gone, with a card and book signed from Mum and Dad, but bought and wrapped by Mum. The winter had passed and spring had arrived but God, I missed Lynette. I missed her so much.

Callum picks up the phone and dials. The phone rings three times and he puts down the receiver. He waits. The phone rings back. Sephy appears holding a phone receiver on the other side of the stage.

Hello, you.

Sephy   Hello, yourself. Code still working then.

Callum   So what're you up to today then?

Sephy   I'm going shopping. With Mother!

Callum   *[Amused]* Poor you.

Sephy   It's not funny.

Callum	Of course not.
Sephy	You're laughing at me again.
Callum	As if.
Sephy	What are you going to do with the rest of the day then?
Callum	I thought I might go to the park, or maybe the beach. Perhaps I'll do both. I haven't decided yet.
Sephy	That's right, rub it in.
Callum	Just think of all that lovely money you're going to spend.
Sephy	Mother's going to spend it, not me. She's decided she needs some retail therapy.
Callum	Well, if you can't get out of it, get into it.
Sephy	I'd much rather be with you.
	Pause.
	Hello?
Callum	Maybe we can meet up later this afternoon.
Sephy	I doubt it. Mum wants to buy me some dresses and update my school uniform and buy herself an evening gown and some shoes. Just the shoes themselves will take three or four hours at least. I swear, Callum, it's going to be torture.
Callum	I might see you at the shopping centre actually. I've got to get some things for school.
Sephy	Like what?
Callum	I was thinking of buying myself a new calculator.
Sephy	I'll keep my eyes open for you. Maybe I'll see you at the café. You can stop me from going completely insane.
Callum	If I miss you at the centre, how about getting together this evening then? We could have a late picnic on the beach.
Sephy	I'll try but I can't guarantee anything.

Callum	Fair enough.
Sephy	Saturday in the Dundale shopping centre. Just shoot me now and put me out of my misery.
Callum	*[Aside]* Lunch that Saturday passed without too much grief – for once. Jude had come from heaven knows where, so we'd all eaten together which made a change.
	Callum *puts his knife and fork down as if he's just finished his meal.*
	I'm off.
Meggie	Where are you going?
Callum	The shopping centre.
Jude	You can't.
Callum	I'll go where I ruddy like. Since when is it any of your business where I go?
Ryan	Callum, I don't want you to go there. Not today.
Meggie	What's going on?
Callum	Why shouldn't I?
	Pause.
	What's wrong with going to the shopping centre?
Ryan	I forbid you to go there, Callum.
Callum	But…
Meggie	What's going on?
	Callum *clicks.*
Callum	*[Aside]* I didn't need to hear any more. I ran out of the house, leaving the front door open.
Jude	Callum –
	Jude *follows* ***Callum*** *off stage.*

SCENE 20

> *Café at the Dundale shopping centre. Cheesy shopping mall music playing in the background.*

Sephy Mother was driving me nuts! In our five long, long hours together, I'd bitten my tongue so many times it'd swollen up to the size of a football. If she asked me for my opinion on one more pair of shoes, I couldn't be responsible for my actions. I sipped my orange juice, grateful for the time alone. She'd gone back to the car park to pack away her various purchases. She was enjoying herself. I'm glad one of us was!

> *Callum charges in.*

Callum Sephy! You've got to get out of here.

Sephy Callum! Where did you spring from?

Callum Never mind that. You've got to leave this place. Right now.

Sephy But I haven't finished my drink.

Callum Never mind your ruddy drink. You have to leave. NOW!

Sephy What's going on?

Callum Don't argue. Out! Come on!

> *An elderly Cross man approaches.*

Man Excuse me, love, but is this boy troubling you?

Sephy No! No. He's a friend of mine. He wants to show me something.

> *Callum drags Sephy out. A loud alarm goes off.*

What's going on?

Callum Move it. Come on.

Sephy *[Aside]* We ran towards the nearest exit. We stumbled out into the spring sunshine and still Callum had hold of my hand and was pulling me after him.

53

Callum	Run. Come on.
Sephy	Where are we going?
Callum	Thank God. It took me almost half an hour to find you. Quick.
Sephy	Callum, I'm getting a stitch.
Callum	Tough. We've got to keep going.
Sephy	Callum, enough!

*She pulls her hand out of his. Suddenly there's a huge explosion. We see **shoppers** blasted in all directions, including **Sephy** and **Callum**. They land, stunned, near one another. A moment of quiet. Then the sound of sirens in the distance, getting louder.*

Mother! Oh my God!

Sephy exits.

● ●

SCENE 21

*At **Callum's** house.*

Callum	Before I knew where I was, I was face to face with Mum.
Meggie	Where have you been? You look terrible. Where's Jude?
Callum	I thought he was here.
Meggie	He and your dad left straight after you. I thought you were all together. You're shaking.
Callum	Haven't you heard?
Meggie	Heard what?

***Callum** picks up the remote and clicks on the TV. The **reporter** comes into the room. A live newsflash. He talks to **Meggie** and **Callum**.*

Reporter	… At least seven people are known to have been killed outright with scores more wounded. Casualties are being taken by ground and air ambulances to local hospitals. The wife and

daughter of Deputy Prime Minister, Kamal Hadley, were reported to have been in the shopping centre at the time but are said to be free from injury.

Meggie	You were with Persephone, weren't you?
Callum	I wanted to buy a new calculator.
Reporter	A warning was received from the Liberation Militia only five minutes before the bomb actually exploded. We have live images from the scene.

*The **reporter** leads **Meggie** and **Callum** around bomb injury victims and rescue workers.*

Moments ago, Kamal Hadley spoke to one of our reporters…

Kamal comes into the room with minder holding an umbrella over Kamal and entourage.

Kamal	If the Liberation Militia think this cowardly, barbaric act of terrorism is going to win over the population of this country to their way of thinking, then they are very much mistaken. All they've done is strengthen our resolve not to give into such people or tactics.

Kamal and entourage leave.

Reporter	A senior police officer on the scene promised that the perpetrators would be brought to swift justice. There will be more information about this in our main news bulletin after the current –

*We hear the front door open. **Ryan** and **Jude** enter. **Meggie** turns off the TV.*

Ryan	What's for supper?

Pause.

Meggie	I'm going to ask you something, Ryan, and I want your solemn promise that you're going to tell me the truth.
Ryan	Not now, Meggie.

He moves to exit into the house. **Meggie** *blocks his way.*

Meggie	Yes. Now. Were you and Jude involved in planting that bomb?
Ryan	I don't know what you're talking about.
Meggie	Damn it, Ryan, don't treat me like an idiot.

Pause.

Ryan	What I did or didn't do is none of your business.
Meggie	Jude, did you have anything to do with this?

***Jude** looks at **Ryan**.*

NO! Don't look at your father. I asked you a question. Now answer it.

Ryan	Jude, keep your mouth shut, d'you hear?
Meggie	I'm still your mother, Jude. Answer me, please.
Jude	We –
Ryan	Jude!
Meggie	Seven people have been killed.
Ryan	What?
Callum	It was on the news.

***Jude** looks at **Ryan**. **Jude** picks up the remote. **Meggie** takes it from him.*

Meggie	Someone better tell me what's going on because we're not leaving this room until I know the truth.
Jude	They were supposed to give a warning.
Meggie	Oh, my God.
Jude	They told us no-one one would be hurt.
Meggie	This isn't happening.
Jude	That everyone would be evacuated.

Meggie	You killed, you *murdered* all those people.
Jude	Something must have gone wrong.
	Meggie is trying to stop herself from retching.
Ryan	No, son, I reckon they planned it this way.
	*Meggie slaps **Ryan's** face. She continues hitting him throughout the next lines.*
Meggie	Ryan, you promised me there'd never be anything like this. You promised you'd only be involved in the background. You promised.
Ryan	*[Restraining her]* I didn't have any choice. Once you're in, they've got you. And you have to do as you're told.
Meggie	You don't. You could've said no. You should've said no.
Ryan	Believe me, I had to do it. I had no choice. I was protecting you, Meggie. And our sons.
Meggie	Protecting us from what? From something you inflicted on us in the first place. You chose to join them.
Ryan	Who do you think I'm doing all this for?
Meggie	I know exactly who you're doing it for. But she's dead, Ryan. And murdering innocent people won't bring her back.
Ryan	You've got it wrong, Meggie.
Meggie	Have I? I warned you, Ryan. I begged you not to involve Jude in all this.
Callum	I'm sure Dad's sorry. Aren't you, Dad? You didn't mean to hurt those people.
Meggie	Sorry? Well he can say that to the families of all those people he's murdered.
Jude	We were told there would be a warning.
Meggie	And what if they had told you there wouldn't be? Would you have refused to be involved then?

Silence.

I can't bear to look at you.

Pause.

Ryan	They were legitimate targets.
Meggie	All those people killed and maimed and that's what you have to offer.
Ryan	How many millions of nought lives have been destroyed by the Crosses over the centuries? No number of people killed in a shopping centre can ever pay for that.
Meggie	These are human beings you're talking about.
Ryan	We're in a state of war, Meggie, and it wasn't the noughts who started it.
Meggie	You've been brainwashed.
Ryan	No, you're the one who's been brainwashed. By the telly and the radio and the newspapers. It's alright for them to use violence when they please, to keep us in poverty and bleed us dry. But when we fight back, they call us cowardly and barbaric.
Meggie	And what about the noughts you just killed? It wasn't only Crosses you know, you killed your own as well.
Ryan	Sometimes the ends have to justify the means. Collateral damage.

Pause.

Meggie	In that case we have nothing more to say to each other. I want you out of this house. I want you out of this house by morning.
Callum	Mum, please.
Ryan	I'm damned if I'll leave my own house.
Meggie	I am not going to let you drag a noose round Jude's neck.

58

Ryan	I'd never let that happen. They'd have to hang me first. I love Jude. That's why I'm in the LM. I want something better for our sons.
Meggie	I'm not arguing with you, Ryan. Just pack your bags and go.
Callum	Let's leave it now. Let's talk it through tomorrow.
Jude	If Dad goes then so do I.
Callum	For God's sake, Jude.
Ryan	No, you won't.
Jude	But you can't stop me belonging to the Liberation Militia. I'm not going to bow out now.
Meggie	Jude, you're a child. You don't know anything.
Jude	I'm actually doing something I can believe in. And I'm not about to give it up. I'm sorry but if you send Dad away I'll just go with him.
Meggie	Then you can both leave.
Callum	Please, Mum, don't.
Meggie	I'll do whatever I have to do to protect Callum. If I can only save one of my children then so be it.
Ryan	Meggie…
Meggie	I don't want you anywhere near me. Don't you ever come near me again.
	Exit Meggie.
Ryan	Meggie…
	Ryan follows Meggie off. Callum stares at Jude.
Callum	It was you, wasn't it? Dad had nothing to do with it.
Jude	He knew what was going on.
Callum	You'd better not let him cover for you.

Jude   Or what?

Jude exits. **Callum** *is left alone. He looks up at the ceiling. He hugs himself.*

Lights fade.

ACT TWO

• •

SCENE 1

Sephy's house. TV room.

Sephy *enters. She holds a TV remote. She introduces her **mother** and **sister** to us. There is an empty chair.*

Sephy   My parents' country house. Seven bedrooms and five reception rooms for four people. What a waste. Four lonely peas rolling about in a cup. More a museum than a home – all cold floors and marble pillars and carved stonework.

Mother: all she ever did was read glossy magazines and drink. Spend time in the gym or the pool and drink. Shop and drink. Every time Mother looked at me, I could feel her wishing that I was more like my scabby big sister, Minerva. I called her Minnie for short when I wanted to annoy her. I called her Minnie all the time.

She goes to the empty chair.

Dad? Dad had found someone else. Her name was Grace and after the next election he was going to make it officially known that he and Mum were no longer together. My family!

Sephy flicks on the TV. The reporter enters.

Reporter   Today, Ryan McGregor of Hugo Yard, Meadowview was formally charged with Political Terrorism and seven counts of murder for the bombing outrage at the Dundale shopping centre. He has confessed to all charges. His family are said to be in hiding.

Minerva   Blanker scumbag!

*Sephy flicks off the TV. **Reporter** exits.*

Sephy   Shut it, Minnie.

Minerva	How many times do I have to tell you not to call me Minnie? My name is Minerva. M-I-N-E-R-V-A! MINERVA!
Sephy	Yes, Minnie.
Minerva	His whole blanker family should swing, not just him.
Jasmine	Minerva, I won't have language like that in this house, d'you hear? You don't live in Meadowview.
Minerva	Yes, mother.

Pause.

	And to think we've had him here, in this very house. And Meggie actually used to be our nanny. If the press put two and two together, they're going to have a field day – and Dad's going to have kittens.
Sephy	What do you mean?
Minerva	Oh, Sephy, use your brain. If Ryan McGregor gets off, Dad will be accused of favouritism and protecting his own and all sorts, whether or not it has anything to do with him. And you haven't helped things by being his son's little lovebird.
Sephy	Say what you like; I know those deaths weren't down to Callum's dad.
Minerva	Nonsense. He's confessed, hasn't he?
Sephy	Who knows what they did to get that confession out of him?
Minerva	Get the message, dur brain. He's a terrorist, end of!
Sephy	Shut it, Minnie.
Minerva	Your boyfriend's family are terrorists. Not a very good judge of character, are we?
Sephy	Mother, they won't really hang him, will they?
Jasmine	If they prove he intended to kill those people, yes.
Sephy	But I know he didn't, Mum. I know him. He's not capable of it.

Minerva	And Callum goes to our school. Dad's going to get it in the neck for that as well.
Sephy	Callum has absolutely nothing to do with this.
Minerva	An apple never falls far from the tree.
Sephy	What a pile of –
Jasmine	Persephone!
Sephy	Even if Ryan McGregor is found guilty – which I don't believe for one second – that doesn't mean that Callum –
Jasmine	Oh, Persephone. Grow up. You're fifteen now. It's about time you stopped behaving like a child.
	Jasmine goes out with her drink.
Sephy	Who put a bee in her knickers?
Minerva	You haven't a clue about the real world, have you?
Sephy	Congratulations. You sound just like Mother.
Minerva	*[Goes to leave]* Take a hike, dog breath.
	Pause.
Sephy	Don't go, Minerva.
	Minerva stops. She turns to Sephy.
Minerva	What?
	Pause.
Sephy	Do you ever feel lonely?
Minerva	Missing your blanker boyfriend, are you?
Sephy	Please, Minerva. Don't be like that.
	Pause.
	Minerva sits down.
	I wish Dad was here. Though he doesn't give a damn about us.

Minerva	That's not true. Dad cares in his own way.
Sephy	Just not as much as he cares about his political career.
	Pause.
Minerva	It's not easy for him with Mum's drinking.
Sephy	Do you think he'll ever come back?
Minerva	Maybe if Mum changes. Gives up the booze.
Sephy	Well that's that then.
	Pause.
	What are we going to do?
Minerva	What can we do?
Sephy	The drinking's getting worse.
Minerva	She's just smoothing over some of the rough edges.
Sephy	Any smoother and she's going to slip over and break her neck.
Minerva	Sephy, if she doesn't want to be helped then there's nothing we can do.
Sephy	I miss her. The person she used to be.
Minerva	We all miss her but this is the way things are. We just have to deal with it.
Sephy	*[Aside]* Maybe Minnie was right. Things are the way they are and one person would never make a difference to a ruddy thing.

● ●

SCENE 2

*In **Mr Stanhope's** office.*

Callum	Mum and I were shown into Mr Stanhope's plush office. His secretary had told Mum it was 'urgent' and 'about the case' but Mum and I both had the same question – 'What case?' The last time we'd seen Mr Stanhope, which was only three

days ago, he's told us quite categorically that he couldn't take Dad on.

Stanhope	Mrs McGregor, Callum, please take a seat.
Meggie	You have some news? Are they going to let Ryan go?
Stanhope	I'm afraid not. Your husband still insists that he's guilty.

Pause.

Callum	He's not. He only confessed because the police threatened to imprison the lot of us. And he's covering. Dad didn't even plant that bomb. We know who did.
Meggie	Callum!
Stanhope	I've been trying to get in touch with you at your home address but there's been no reply.
Meggie	We're staying with my sister, Charlotte, on the other side of Meadowview.
Stanhope	You've been getting hate letters?
Callum	*[Aside]* Amongst other things. Like bricks through the window and death threats.
Stanhope	Well, I'm happy to tell you that I will be able to take on your husband's case. And the really good news is, I've persuaded Kelani Adams QC to be your barrister – not that she took much persuading.
Meggie	I can't afford a barrister like Kelani Adams.
Stanhope	Don't worry about that. Her fees are all taken care of.
Callum	What does that mean?
Stanhope	It means that you don't have to worry about the money.
Meggie	I'd appreciate it if you answered my son's question properly.
Stanhope	An anonymous benefactor has stepped forward with a very generous sum of money, to ensure that your husband gets the fairest trial possible.

Meggie	We don't take charity, Mr Stanhope.
Stanhope	It's not charity. I was told to inform you of that in the strongest possible terms.
Meggie	By who?
Callum	Does it matter, Mum?
Stanhope	As I said, I received a banker's cheque and a typewritten, unsigned note with several instructions.
Meggie	May we see the note?
Callum	What's the point?
Stanhope	I'm afraid not. One of the conditions was that you shouldn't be allowed to see it.
Meggie	Well, I'm sorry. We can't accept it.
Callum	We can't afford not to.
Meggie	How do we know where this money's come from, Callum?
Stanhope	Mrs McGregor, this is your husband's one and only chance. I would strongly advise you to take it.
Callum	Mum, I think we should do whatever it takes to save Dad's life. It doesn't matter where the money came from. We have to do what we can. We've just got to swallow our pride.
	Pause.
Meggie	OK then.
Callum	I knew who had sent the money to Mr Stanhope. I had no idea how she'd done it. And I had even less idea how I was ever going to thank her, never mind repay her. But I would. I sat in Mr Stanhope's office, on his expensive brown leather chair and swore an oath before God that I would pay Sephy back. If it took me every penny I earned for the rest of my life, I would repay her.

SCENE 3

	Sephy's house.
Sephy	I came home from school and got the shock of my life. Dad's suitcases were in the hallway.
	*Enter **Kamal**. **Jasmine** follows, for the moment unseen by **Sephy**. She is holding a large glass of wine.*
Kamal	Hello, Princess.
	*Sephy runs up to **Kamal** and hugs him.*
Sephy	Dad! I've missed you.
Kamal	I've missed you, too.
	He swings her around.
	Good grief! What have you been eating? You weigh a ton!
Sephy	Thanks a bunch! Are you staying for good?
Kamal	For a while at least.
	*Sephy clocks **Jasmine**.*
Sephy	What… What's going on?
Jasmine	Ask your father. He has all the answers.
	Pause.
Sephy	Oh, I get it. You're only here for the trial. Aren't you?
	*Enter **Minerva**, dressed very smartly.*
Minerva	Ready!
	*Enter **Juno**, Kamal's PR.*
Juno	We thought the front steps would be best. You must be Persephone.
	*She offers **Sephy** her hand.*

Sephy	Hello.
Juno	Juno Aylette. Your father's PR. But we have to get a move on I'm afraid. The light's fading.
Kamal	We'll be right out.
Juno	Great. What beautiful girls. They won't need much in the way of make-up.
Sephy	What's going on?
Kamal	Just a quick family photo, Princess. Thanks, Juno, we'll be out in a moment.
Juno	Sure.

Juno exits.

Minerva	We're going to be in the Sunday papers. How cool is that?
Sephy	What?
Jasmine	Let's just get it over with.
Kamal	You'd better get changed, Princess.
Minerva	Something smart but relaxed.
Sephy	No way.
Kamal	Come on, sweetheart. Then we can go out for supper. Celebrate me being home.
Sephy	I'm not doing it, Dad. I don't care how many times you ask. I'm not going to play happy family for the cameras. You'll have to boost your poll ratings without me.
Kamal	But they want the whole family, Princess.

Juno comes back in.

Juno	Mr Hadley, the light…
Minerva	Come on, Dad. Let's do it without her.
Kamal	[*To Sephy*] Suit yourself, young lady.

*They go to exit, leaving **Sephy**.*

Kamal	Your glass, Jasmine.
Jasmine	Oh.

*Juno, Minerva and **Kamal** exit. **Jasmine** takes a swig of the wine and gives it to **Sephy**.*

Pop this in the fridge for me, darling.

Kamal	*[From offstage]* Jasmine! Hurry up.
Juno	*[Confidentially]* I don't blame you for not joining in.

***Jasmine** goes.*

***Sephy** looks at the glass of wine. She goes towards it, picks up the glass and sniffs it. She brings it to her lips and takes a long swig. She pauses. Takes another swig, then finishes the glass.*

• •

SCENE 4

Headmaster's office, Heathcroft school.

Callum   I'd seen a lot of plush offices this week. First Mr Stanhope's, now Mr Corsa our headmaster's. Stepping onto his carpet felt like walking on spring grass.

Mr Corsa   Ah, Callum. Come in. Sit down, please.

***Callum** sits.*

Callum, there's no easy way to say this so I'm going to get right to the point.

Callum   Yes, sir?

Mr Corsa   Until the matter regarding your father is satisfactorily resolved, the governors and I have decided that it would serve everyone's best interests if you were suspended for a while.

Callum   I'm guilty til my dad's proven innocent? Is that it?

Mr Corsa   Callum, I do hope you're going to be reasonable about this.

69

Callum	Should I empty my locker now or will the end of the day be soon enough?
Mr Corsa	That's entirely up to you.
Callum	You must be delighted. Two down, only one more to go.
Mr Corsa	Meaning?
Callum	Meaning Colin has gone and you couldn't wait to get rid of Shania and now it's my turn.
Mr Corsa	Shania was expelled for gross misconduct.
Callum	Shania only slapped Gardner Wilson because he hit her first. And everyone knows that including you. How come Shania gets expelled and Gardner gets away with a telling off? Why isn't it gross misconduct when a Cross does it?
Mr Corsa	I have no intention of justifying school policy to you. We'll be happy to review your situation once the trial is over and the dust clears.
Callum	But the dust is never going to clear, is it? And we both know that.

Mr Corsa holds out his hand. Callum looks at it.

Mr Corsa	Good luck to you, Callum.
Callum	*[Aside]* I turned back and slammed the door as hard as I could. A childish gesture I know. But it felt so good.
Mr Corsa	Callum, come here!
Callum	I carried on walking.
Mr Corsa	I said, come back here.
Callum	I wasn't part of his school anymore. I didn't have to do what he said. I wasn't part of the whole Cross way of life. Why should I do what any of them said? I was out of Heathcroft. And I was never coming back.

SCENE 5

Sephy's house.

After checking to see that no-one is watching, **Sephy** *secretly pours a glass of wine. She goes to drink it. She stops.*

Sephy I limit myself to one glass a night. I don't like the taste particularly. But it makes me feel better. Kind of warm and careless. It smoothes out the rough edges. I don't mind so much about Mother or Father or Minerva anymore. I don't even mind about Callum. Isn't that cool?

SCENE 6

The trial.

Callum When they brought me into the courtroom I could see my father to the right. The judge was droning on and on at the jury, telling them what the case was about and what it was not about. Twelve good men and women. Twelve good Cross men and women, of course. How else could justice be served? I looked down at the Good Book under my hand. It was cool, almost cold beneath my fingers. 'The truth?'. Which version of the truth will this Cross court find acceptable?

Mr Pingule stands.

Mr Pingule Callum, what's your opinion of the Liberation Militia?

Callum I… any organization which promotes equality between noughts and Crosses is… Noughts and Crosses should be equal… I support anyone who tries to bring that about.

Mr Pingule So neither you or anyone in your family knew anything about the planting of the bomb at the Dundale shopping centre?

Callum No.

Mr Pingule Well, can you tell me what you were doing in the Dundale approximately ten minutes before the bomb went off?

Callum	*[Aside]* I watched as a TV with a massive screen and a VCR were wheeled into the court.
Mr Pingule	In this film, who are you pulling from the Cuckoo's Egg café?
Callum	Sephy…
Mr Pingule	I'm sorry, what was that?
Callum	Persephone Hadley.
Mr Pingule	What is your relationship with Persephone Hadley?
Callum	She's… She's a friend.
Mr Pingule	Could you tell me why you were in such a hurry to get Persephone out of there, just before the bomb went off?
Callum	I was late and I was afraid her mum would appear at any second and… I wanted to show her something.
Mr Pingule	What was that?
Callum	Something silly.
	Pause.
	With everything that's happened, I can't remember.
Mr Pingule	No further questions.
	Mr Pingule *sits.*
Callum	*[Aside]* Forgive me, Dad, please forgive me.
Sephy	*[Aside]* I don't know how Callum's mum managed to get Kelani Adams to defend Mr McGregor but I was so glad she had. Even I'd heard of Kelani Adams. According to the telly, Kelani was making sure that the trial was as fair as possible.
Kelani	Could you describe your relationship with Mrs Hadley, Persephone Hadley's mother?
Callum	Mrs Hadley… doesn't much like me.
Kelani	Callum, what would you have done if Persephone had been in the café with her mother?

Callum	*[Aside]* How should I answer? Think! Think!
Kelani	Yes, Callum?
Callum	I would have waited until Sephy was alone before trying to speak to her.
Kelani	But it might have taken a while before you got to tell Sephy what you wanted to tell her?
Callum	Yes.
Kelani	Is that why you were in such a hurry?
Callum	It was.
Kelani	Thank you, Callum. That will be all.
	Kelani *sits.*
Sephy	*[Aside]* Ryan McGregor just had to be found not guilty. It was only right and proper.
Callum	*[Aside]* Good or bad, every aspect of my life lay in the hands of others. Kelani Adams; the teachers at Heathcroft; now the jury.
Sephy	*[Aside]* Ryan wasn't guilty. So why did I feel like I was the only person in the world – the only Cross in the world to believe that?
Callum	*[Aside]* Maybe this was it. Maybe this was all there was or would ever be to my life.
Sephy	*[Aside]* But justice simply had to be done. The jury would see the truth.
Callum	*[Aside]* Mum and I held hands as we waited for the foreman to speak. Hope and hopelessness churned in my stomach like oil and water.
Clerk	D'you find the defendant, Ryan McGregor, guilty or not guilty of the crime of political terrorism?
Callum	*[Aside]* Why was the foreman taking so long to speak? Answer the question… What's your answer? Why couldn't I hear anything?

Clerk	Do you find the defendant, Ryan McGregor, guilty or not guilty of the crime of first degree murder?
Callum	*[Aside]* And I heard the verdict that time. God help me, I heard it.

SCENE 7

Sephy's garden.

Sephy	I sat on the garden swing. I didn't actually swing any more – that was kid's stuff. I just… twisted. I'd come home and gone straight out into the garden. For the two weeks after the trial Mother had got worse so now I just did what I was told and kept my head down. And for the most part it worked.
Jasmine	*[Offstage]* Sephy, what are you doing?
Sephy	*[To audience]* Uh-oh! Trouble!
Jasmine	Come here, please.
Sephy	*[Aside]* I ran into the house.
	Enter Jasmine.

Jasmine	Go to your room and put on your navy-blue dress and your blue shoes.
Sephy	My Jackson Spacey?
Jasmine	Be downstairs in five minutes. We need to be on our way by half-past four.
Sephy	Where are we going?
Jasmine	Never you mind.
Sephy	Why do I have to get dressed up?
Jasmine	Because I said so. Do as you're told. And tell your sister to hurry up as well.
Sephy	But why?
Jasmine	Just get a move on, please.

*Sephy changes into the dress she wore at **Lynette's** wake.*

Sephy	I knew it was something major when Dad was standing in the driveway next to his official government Mercedes. I hadn't seen him since the trial finished. Ten to six and our car drew up outside Hewmett prison. And only then, when it'd been spelt out for me, did I finally realize what I was doing there.

• •

SCENE 8

*Prison execution chamber. A gallows. **Callum** and family; **Sephy** and family. A crowd of noughts on one side and a **crowd of Crosses** on the other. The **reporter** is also present and taking notes.*

Clerk	Ladies and gentlemen and noughts, we are here today to witness the execution of Ryan McGregor of 15 Hugo Yard, Meadowview, having been found guilty of seven counts of murder and the charge of political terrorism. The sentence will now be carried out of hanging by the neck until he is dead.
Sephy	[To audience] I didn't know, Callum.
Clerk	Bring in the prisoner.

*A guard brings **Ryan** in. **Sephy** looks at **Callum**.*

Sephy	*[Aside]* How to make my desperate thoughts reach him? I swear I didn't know, Callum. I wouldn't have come if I'd known where we were going. Wild horses couldn't have dragged me through those gates. That's the truth. Callum, you must believe that.
Clerk	*[To **Ryan**]* Do you have anything to say?
Sephy	Mother, I want to leave.

Ryan shakes his head. An executioner covers his head completely with a hood.

Jasmine	Not now, Sephy.
Sephy	*[Standing]* I want to leave – NOW.
Jasmine	Sit down, Persephone, and stop making an exhibition of yourself.
Sephy	Nothing is going to make me sit here and watch this. I'm leaving.

*She goes to leave. **Jasmine** grabs her.*

Jasmine	Now sit down and don't say another word.

Sephy sits down. The prison clock chimes four times. Then, on the fifth –

Ryan	Long live the Liberation Militia!

*The **prison governor** enters.*

Governor	Wait! Wait!

The clock strikes six.

	Ladies and gentlemen and noughts, I am Governor Giustini. I have just been informed that Ryan McGregor has received a reprieve. His sentence has been commuted to life imprisonment.
Ryan	Long live the…

Ryan collapses but is caught by the guard and led out. The
noughts *riot (continuing throughout **Callum's** speech).*

Callum   We could have torn down Hewmett Prison brick by brick. We
would've. I turned to where they were sitting. I couldn't see
her. Where was she? Watching all this and enjoying the free
entertainment? At that precise moment I felt like I could rip
the metal barriers out of the concrete beneath my feet with my
bare hands. Someone grabbed my arm. It was Mum. And just
like that all my anger subsided. I stood watching Mum. Waiting
for the pain inside to dampen down. Waiting for the world
around me to turn multi-coloured again. Instead of blood red.

*The **Hadleys** leave. The crowd melts away.*

• •

SCENE 9

*Sephy's house. The kitchen. **Jasmine** pours herself a glass of wine
from a Chardonnay bottle.*

Sephy   *[To **Jasmine**]* Don't you ever, ever do that to me again!

Jasmine   Calm down please, young lady.

Sephy   How could you take me to that… thing? How could you?

Jasmine   We didn't have a choice. It was our duty.

Sephy   Our duty? To sit and watch a man get hanged?

Jasmine   Yes. We have a duty to support your father, whether we agree
with what he's doing or not.

Sephy   That was… barbaric. Taking us to watch a man die. Dad's sick.
So are you.

Jasmine   I didn't like it any more than you did.

Sephy   Liar. You couldn't take your eyes off it.

Jasmine   I couldn't even look.

*As **Jasmine** goes to pour another glass of wine, **Sephy** snatches the
half-empty bottle from her.*

	Give me that bottle.
Sephy	Or what?
Jasmine	Persephone, give me that bottle. Now.

Sephy throws the bottle across the floor and it smashes.

Go to your room.

Sephy	You couldn't care less, could you? You would have cared more if they were hanging a wine bottle instead of a person.

Jasmine slaps Sephy.

Jasmine	How dare you speak to me like that.
Sephy	There's wine spilling out over there. Go and lick it up then. You wouldn't want to waste any, would you?

Pause.

Waiting for me to leave before you get on your hands and knees? OK then. I'll leave you to it.

Jasmine grabs Sephy and turns her round.

Jasmine	You don't know every damn thing, Persephone. You think you're the only one in pain here? Ryan McGregor was my friend. So was Meggie. Do you think I wanted to watch him hang?
Sephy	You still went.
Jasmine	One day you'll realize that you can't always do what you want in this life. And when you realize that, maybe you'll stop judging me.
Sephy	I want to think of you as little as possible.
Jasmine	Oh, grow up.
Sephy	You say they were your friends? Nothing would make me go to the hanging of one of my friends. Nothing. Not even Dad.
Jasmine	I tried to help.
Sephy	How? By getting drunk.

Jasmine	Who d'you think paid for their all their legal fees, you stupid girl?
	Pause.
Sephy	I don't believe you.
Jasmine	I did everything that was humanly possible to make sure Ryan McGregor wouldn't hang. And that's not to leave this room.
	Pause.
Sephy	If you did, it was only because of your guilty conscience. You've never done anything for another human being in your life.
Jasmine	Well, I brought you and your sister up.
Sephy	No, that was Meggie McGregor.
Jasmine	Meggie McGregor looked after you because she was paid. And paid well. Maybe, when you have a daughter of your own, you'll find out that being a mother is not as easy as it seems. Life can be very cruel and very lonely. But I suppose you haven't learned that yet.
Sephy	Oh, go back to your bottle. You deserve each other.

Sephy runs to her room and gets out a bottle of alcohol. She takes the lid off and goes to drink it. She stops. She throws the bottle away. At the same time, we see Jasmine clearing up the mess from the kitchen floor.

• •

SCENE 10

Prison visiting room.

Callum	*[Aside]* Two hours and a lot of arguing from our solicitor later, we were finally allowed into the visiting room to see Dad.
Officer	You've got five minutes.
Ryan	I hear they're blaming me for the riot.
Meggie	How are you?

Pause.

Well, at least we can be grateful for the reprieve.

Ryan   They should have hanged me. It would have been kinder.

Meggie   Don't say that.

Ryan   Why not? Do you really think I want to spend the rest of my life locked up in this hellhole?

Kelani enters.

Kelani   We've won the first battle. Onto the next one. I've already launched the appeal.

Ryan   With all due respect, Miss Adams, this is as far as you'll get.

Kelani   Oh no, it's not. I'm calling in every favour I'm owed.

Ryan   I don't want to appeal, Miss Adams, I haven't got the strength. I think that we both know that I'll never see the outside of this prison again.

Pause.

Meggie   That's not true.

Pause.

Kelani   You need some time to think it over.

Ryan   The only way I'm leaving this place is in a box. Hopefully sooner rather than later.

Meggie   For God's sake, Ryan. Callum's here.

Kelani   I'll come back in a few days, see how you're feeling then.

Ryan   I won't feel any different.

Callum   Please think about it, Dad.

Ryan   How's Heathcroft, son?

Pause.

Callum   It's fine, Dad. All fine.

Ryan	That's great news. You make sure you get good results.
Callum	I'll do my best.
Ryan	I'm very proud of you, son.
Officer	That's it. Visiting time is over.
Meggie	See you next week, love.
Callum	Bye, Dad.
Ryan	I'm expecting 'A's, Callum. Straight 'A's.

*Officer removes **Ryan**.*

Kelani	I'm sure he'll come round. It's quite natural to feel despondent after what he's been through.
Meggie	He didn't even say goodbye.

• •

SCENE 11

*Dining room, **Sephy's** house.*

Sephy	The night the TV showed Callum's house burned to the ground I went to my bedroom and cried and cried. I wanted to phone but I didn't have his new number. I wanted to visit but I didn't have his new address. I still went to the beach once in a while but he was never there. I pretended to myself that we just kept missing each other. I'd arrive at five, he'd arrive at six. I'd arrive at six, he'd arrive at seven. But deep down, I knew that he'd stopped coming. He had more important things on his mind. When the trial ended I went back to seeing more of Dad on the telly than I did in the flesh. I suspected something fishy was going on when his car pulled outside the house in time for dinner one evening.

Sephy, Minerva, Kamal and Jasmine sit at dinner. They eat in silence.

Kamal	So how's school going, Princess?
Sephy	[Aside] Princess? Definitely fishy!

Kamal	Mother tells me your results have been good.
Sephy	Heathcroft's fine, Dad. Fairly boring, actually.
Kamal	I worry sometimes that Heathcroft doesn't quite stretch you enough.
Sephy	It's a good school. Loads of people move here to get their kids in.
Kamal	Look, I'm concerned – your mother and I are concerned – about how things will go for you there now that Ryan McGregor's been convicted.
Sephy	Why would things be bad for me? Why would they be worse for me than for Minerva?
Kamal	I think we all know why.
Sephy	I'm afraid my telepathic powers aren't what they used to be.
Jasmine	Please don't be cheeky, Persephone.
Kamal	When you were attacked by those girls, it happened because of your friendship with the McGregor boy.
Sephy	It happened because those girls were ignorant bigots. And his name's Callum. Anyway, you don't need to worry about him, they've booted him out along with the other noughts who dared to believe they were entitled to a decent education.
Kamal	We think it would be better if we took you out of Heathcroft. We've made enquiries at Chivers. They have a place and they could take you in next term.
Sephy	But I don't want to go to boarding school. I like it at Heathcroft.
Kamal	Your mother and I are in complete agreement on this. Aren't we, Jasmine?
Jasmine	It's all for the best, darling. And Chivers is one of the best schools in the country.
Sephy	So what? This has nothing to do with my education. You're just

	frightened that the TV and the ruddy newspapers will find out that Meggie used to work for us. As usual, it's about your ruddy career.
Jasmine	Watch your language, young lady.
Kamal	I want to get you away from the McGregors and everything they stand for.
Sephy	But Callum had nothing to do with Dundale. It's his father that's been convicted, not him.
Kamal	That won't matter to the thugs, Princess. They know you as a friend of the McGregor's. I trust you saw what they did to his house.
Minerva	He's thinking about you, Sephy.
Sephy	You won't make me go. I'll refuse. I'll leave home and move in with Callum.
Kamal	You do that and I'll cut you off without a penny.
Sephy	I couldn't care less. We'll go away together. Go up north. Start a new life.
Kamal	How do you propose to pay for that?
Sephy	I'll work.
Kamal	I'm afraid we've made the decision and we're not going to change our minds. In September, you're going to Chivers and that's the end of it.
	He gets up.
Jasmine	*[To Kamal]* You're not leaving now, surely?
Kamal	The PM's called a security summit.
Sephy	*[Aside]* Dinner with Grace more like.
Kamal	It'll all work out, Princess. Trust me.
	Kamal *goes to kiss* **Sephy**. *She pulls away. He goes to leave.*
Jasmine	Please stay and finish your meal, Kamal. For the girls.

SCENE 11   ACT 2

83

Kamal	Look, I told her myself. That's what you wanted, wasn't it?
Jasmine	I was hoping you might want to spend some time with your daughters.
Kamal	I'll see them next week.
Jasmine	When?
Kamal	I'll have to check my diary.
Jasmine	Perhaps you'd like me to call your PA. Arrange an appointment.
Kamal	If you were sober enough to remember, that might be a good idea.
	[To Sephy] It'll all work out, Princess. Trust me.
	***Kamal** goes to kiss **Sephy** on the forehead. She pulls away. He goes to exit.*
Sephy	Send our love to Gracey!
	He goes.
Jasmine	I know it's hard for you, darling, but maybe boarding school will be an adventure.
Sephy	I thought you said you cried yourself to sleep every night you were there.
Jasmine	Well I was only eight when I started. But at your age it's different. You'll make friends and I'm sure you'll grow to love it.
Sephy	More to the point, I'll be out of your hair.
Jasmine	You know that's not true, Sephy. I'll miss you terribly.
Sephy	Good thing Dad's not sending your Chardonnay supplier away. Then you'd be in real trouble.
Jasmine	What a lovely family meal! We must do it more often.
	Jasmine goes.
Minerva	You're not seriously thinking of running off with that blanker.

Sephy	Just watch me.
Minerva	You haven't got the nerve.

● ●

SCENE 12

Sephy's room. Night time. The sound of pebbles on a window.
Sephy goes to her window.

Sephy — It must have been two o'clock in the morning. It took a while before I heard the strange tip-tapping at my window. And once I was conscious of it, I realized that it'd been going on for a while. I headed for my balcony window and opened it. Tiny stones lay at my feet

Callum — *[Offstage]* Sephy.

Sephy — What? How did you get through security?

Callum — *[Offstage]* I need to see you.

Sephy — I'll come down. It's safer.

Callum — *[Offstage]* No. I'll climb up.

Sephy — Hang on, I'll tie some sheets together then.

Callum — *[Offstage]* No, don't bother.

Sephy — *[Offstage as he climbs up]* Be quick. The place is crawling with guards. Watch it… Mind the living room window… No. Get your left hand over the balcony. That's it.

Callum enters through the window.

Did you phone me? I didn't hear your signal.

Callum — I was in the prison with my dad.

Pause as Callum and Sephy take each other in.

Sephy — How's your mum?

Callum — She's at my aunt's house.

Sephy goes to her bedroom door and locks it.

Sephy	They're sending me away to boarding school. In September. The thirteenth. Unlucky for some.
Callum	Well that's the end of us, I suppose.
Sephy	It doesn't have to be.
Callum	Come off it, Sephy.
Sephy	Remember that time on the beach? The night before you started at Heathcroft? You talked about us going away together. Escaping. Remember?

Pause.

Well, how about it? I've got plenty of money. And we can both work. We could move right away from here. Maybe rent a place up north somewhere. Maybe in the country.

Pause.

Callum	Your father must be happy. My dad rots away in prison and just like that, Kamal Hadley's reputation is restored. Is this the way it's going to be from now on? Whenever a politician is in trouble in the polls they'll just search out the nearest nought to put away or string up – or both? Cheaper than starting a war, I suppose.
Sephy	I know your dad didn't kill those people.
Callum	Do you know how long the jury deliberated? One hour. One lousy, stinking hour.

Sephy *touches* **Callum's** *cheek.*

Sephy	I'm so sorry, Callum.

Callum *pulls his head away.*

Callum	*[Raising his voice]* I don't want your ruddy pity.
Sephy	Stop it. Please.
Callum	*[Still shouting]* Why should I? Don't you want anyone to know you've got a blanker in your room?

Sephy	Callum, don't.
Callum	I want to smash you and every other dagger who crosses my path. I hate you so much it scares me.
Sephy	I know you do. You've hated me ever since you joined Heathcroft and I called you a blanker.
Callum	And you've hated me for turning my back on you in the dining hall and letting you be beaten up by those girls.

Pause.

Then why is it that I think of you as my best friend?

Sephy	Because you know that's how I think of you. Because I love you. And you love me, I think.

Pause.

Did you hear what I said? I love you.

Callum	Love doesn't exist; friendship doesn't exist between a nought and a Cross.
Sephy	Then what are you doing in my room?
Callum	I'm damned if I know.

*Sephy sits on the bed. **Callum** sits alongside her but some distance away. They are both very uncomfortable. They look at the floor. Then **Sephy** turns to **Callum** and offers her hand. He turns to her. She starts to lower her hand. He takes it and moves towards her. We hear the gentle sound of waves on the beach. They sit like this for a few moments. Then he kicks off his shoes and lies down on the bed, taking her with him. They hug.*

Turn around.

Sephy does. They spoon together.

Are you OK?

Sephy	Uh-hm.
Callum	I'm not squashing you?

Sephy	Uh-uh.
Callum	You're sure.
Sephy	Callum, shut up.

Callum smiles. Sephy turns to face him. They kiss. Sephy pulls away.

Let's just get some sleep – OK?

Callum	OK.

They curl up.

Sephy.

Sephy	Mmmm.
Callum	Maybe we should go away together.

Sephy's nodding off.

Sephy	We'll talk about it in the morning.

Pause.

Callum	I remember years ago when you snuck me my first taste of orange juice. It was icy-cold and I'd never tasted anything so sweet and I held each sip in my mouth until it became warm because I couldn't bear to swallow it. I wanted the taste to last forever but of course it couldn't.

Silence.

Sephy, I want to tell you something.

Silence.

A secret.

Silence.

Sephy?

He realizes she's asleep and gives up. They lie still together. The light slowly fades and the scene goes from night to morning as they sleep. Dawn chorus.

SCENE 13

	Sephy's bedroom. Midday. We hear offstage knocking at the door. *Sephy starts to wake up.*
Sarah	*[Offstage]* Miss Sephy? It's Sarah and your mother. Are you all right in there?
Jasmine	*[Offstage]* Persephone, open this door. At once.
	Sarah knocks again.
	[Offstage] Persephone, open the door right this second or I'll get security to break it down.
Sarah	*[Offstage]* Miss Sephy, are you OK? Please.
Sephy	Just… a minute.
	*She shakes **Callum** awake.*
Callum	What… What's the?
	*Sarah knocks on the door again. **Sephy** puts her hand over **Callum's** mouth. She points towards the door. He goes to get under the bed.*
Sephy	*[Whispering]* Look, why don't I just let them in? I want my mother to know about us. Besides, we haven't done anything wrong.
	***Callum** looks at her.*
	Bad idea?
Callum	Dur!
	*He disappears under the bed. **Sephy** goes to put her dressing gown on over her Jackson Spacey dress. More knocking.*
Sephy	I'm on my way, Sarah. I'm just putting on my dressing gown.
	*She rushes to the door and unlocks it. **Jasmine** bustles past her into the room. **Sarah** follows. **Jasmine** goes to the window and looks out.*

	What's the matter? Is the house on fire?
Jasmine	D'you know what time it is?
Sephy	So I overslept a few minutes. Big deal.
Sarah	It's almost noon and your door is locked.
Sephy	Maybe I decided to bring a little excitement into your lives.

Sephy notices Callum's hand reaching out from under the bed to retrieve his trainers, which are on Sephy and Sarah's side of the bed. He grabs a trainer and removes it.

	I'll be down as soon as I've had my shower. I promise.
Jasmine	There's nothing wrong?
Sephy	'Course not. What could be wrong?

Sarah turns to leave and notices Callum's remaining trainer.

| Jasmine | You're hiding something. I know it. |
| Sephy | Just 'cause I overslept? |

Sarah heads towards the trainer.

Sarah, what...?

Sarah surreptitiously kicks the trainer under the bed. Then covers by tidying Sephy's bedclothes.

Jasmine	My daughter is quite capable of making her own bed, Sarah.
Sarah	Yes, Mrs Hadley.
Jasmine	[To Sephy] I'm watching you.

Jasmine goes off to the door and exits. Sarah follows. Just before exiting, she checks to see that Jasmine has cleared, then turns back to Sephy.

| Sarah | [Whispering] Get Callum dressed and out of here! |

She exits and we hear her shutting the door.

| Sephy | You can come out now. |

Callum sticks his head out and they both burst out laughing.

Callum	Just your ordinary average Sunday morning.
Sephy	Never a dull moment.

Callum starts writing something on a piece of paper.

What's that?

Callum	The address at my aunt's. You can contact me there. If you're serious about going away, you'll know where to find me. I'd better go.

They kiss. He exits. She gets on the bed and turns on the TV. The reporter enters.

Reporter	Ryan McGregor, the convicted bomber of the Dundale shopping centre was killed this morning whilst trying to escape from Hewmett Prison. He died whilst attempting to scale the electrified fence surrounding the prison. McGregor was due to hang yesterday but received a dramatic last minute reprieve from the Home Office. His family are said to be devastated at the news and were unavailable for comment. Officials have launched an immediate inquiry. A statement was issued today saying that suicide would not be ruled out as the official cause of –

Sephy flicks the TV off with the remote and the reporter exits.

● ●

SCENE 14

Sephy's house. Sarah Pike's office.

Sephy	The summer passed by in a blur and before long it was the 12th of September. The day before I was due to go to Chivers. It was now or never.

Sephy puts a letter in an envelope and goes to Sarah.

Morning, Sarah, I… Could you do me a favour? A really big one.

Sarah	Oh, yes? What's that then?

Sephy	Could you deliver this letter to Callum McGregor? Today? He's staying with his aunt. I've written the address on the front.
Sarah	I don't think so. I can't afford to lose this job.
Sephy	Please, Sarah. I'm begging you. It's really important.
	Pause.
Sarah	You're not pregnant are you?
	Sephy laughs.
	I guess not.
Sephy	Please. I wouldn't ask you if it wasn't really, really important.
Sarah	OK. I'll deliver it on my way home tonight. And only on one condition.
Sephy	What's that?
Sarah	That you don't do anything… hasty.
Sephy	It's a deal.

She hugs Sarah. Sephy hands Sarah the letter. Sarah exits.

[To audience] Hasty? Hasty? I'd thought and considered and planned this for days, weeks, months, all my life. Callum would read my letter and come for me and together we were going to escape. Tomorrow.

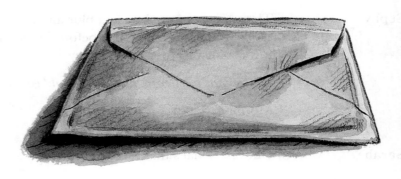

Burger bar. **Callum** sits with his drink.

Callum   The days stretched before me like a never-ending desert. They'd killed... they'd murdered my dad in July and it was now September. When Dad died, something inside me had died as well. Although the weeks had come and gone, it still cut like a knife every time I thought of him. I hadn't heard from Sephy since the Saturday night-Sunday morning I spent with her. All that talk about running away. Fairy tales. And tomorrow was the day she was leaving for boarding school. They were right – love doesn't exist between a nought and a Cross. And it never would.

Enter **Jude** behind **Callum**.

Jude   Hello, little brother.

Callum   Jude!

Callum jumps up and hugs **Jude**.

I've missed you.

Jude   Get off. Are you mad or what?

He glances around and sits down with **Callum**.

Stop grinning like an idiot!

Callum   It's great to see you! Where've you been? I really have missed you.

Jude   I've been keeping my head down for a while.

Callum   You know about Dad?

Jude   Of course. And now it's payback time.

Callum   What d'you mean?

Pause.

Jude   I hear they booted you out of Heathcroft.

Callum	I wasn't booted. I walked.
Jude	Good for you. That wasn't the place for you, little brother.
Callum	I know that now.
Jude	It's a shame you didn't listen to me when I told you months ago. It would've saved you a lot of grief.

Callum shrugs.

So what're you up to these days?

Callum	Let's put it this way, hanging around in burger bars is the highlight.
Jude	Would you like to do something more worthwhile?
Callum	Like what?
Jude	I have to go now. Someone will be in touch.
Callum	Jude, don't do your man of mystery routine on me. What am I meant to tell Mum?
Jude	Don't tell her anything. Where we're going, she can't follow.
Callum	And where are we going?
Jude	I think you know, little brother.
Callum	Stop calling me that. What're you up to Jude?
Jude	Just tell me one thing. Are you in or out?

Pause.

Well?

Pause.

This is your chance to make a difference.

Callum	I'm in.
Jude	Go home, pack your bags and make your peace with Mum. Report to this address at seven o'clock tonight. After that you won't be seeing Mum or anyone else you know for a while.

Callum	No-one at all?
Jude	No. Are you still in?

Callum nods.

Welcome to the lifeboat party, little brother. I hope I can trust you.

• •

SCENE 16

Callum's bedroom at his aunt's house.

Callum packs a suitcase on one side of the stage and Sephy does the same on the other. Enter Meggie. She's aged considerably.

Meggie	What're you doing?
Callum	I'm going away.
Meggie	I see.

Pause.

Will you stay for your tea?

Callum	No, I'd best be off now, Mum.

Pause.

Meggie	When will you be back?
Callum	I don't know.
Meggie	I suppose you'll be seeing your brother
Callum	I don't know. Probably.
Meggie	How is he?

Pause.

You know I don't want you to go.

Callum	Apart from you I've got nothing to keep me here. And I need to do something for Dad.

Meggie	And he needed to do something for your sister. Where does it stop, Callum? When they've killed the lot of us?
Callum	It's up to them to stop it first.
Meggie	It's up to all of us.
	Pause.
	Do one thing for me.
Callum	What's that?
Meggie	Keep your head down. And tell your brother to do the same.
Callum	OK, Mum. I'll go out the back.
	Callum exits. Pause. Meggie is devastated. The doorbell rings. She gathers herself and goes offstage to answer the door.
Meggie	Hello, Sarah.
Sarah	I've got a letter for Callum. Is he in?
Meggie	He's just gone out.

• •

SCENE 17

Sephy's bedroom. The sound of rain outside. Sephy finishes packing. She goes to the window.

Sephy	He's coming. He's not going to come. He's coming. He's not going to come. He's –
Jasmine	*[Offstage]* Persephone, move it. The car's waiting.
Sephy	I'm coming! *[She goes to the window]* Where is he?
	Minerva enters.
Minerva	Enjoy yourself, Sephy.
Sephy	Take care of Mum.
	Minerva nods. Pause.
Minerva	You lay off the booze, OK?

Sephy	I'll try.
Minerva	You better. I haven't got the energy to look after two of you.
Jasmine	*[Offstage]* Sephy, please hurry up!
Minerva	Bye, then.
	*Minerva leans forward and awkwardly kisses **Sephy** on the cheek. **Minerva** exits. **Sephy** looks through the window.*
Jasmine	*[Offstage]* Sephy!
	She closes her case. She goes to look out of the window.
Sephy	*[To herself]* He's not coming.
	She picks up her case and leaves.
	OK, Mother.
	Sound of front door closing. Car door slams. Car starts up and drives off.

● ●

SCENE 18

Sephy's house.

Sephy	I'd finished my end-of-year exams and the summer holidays had already started. Over two and a half years away from home and to be honest, I had no desire whatsoever to return. But this time Mother wasn't taking no for an answer. I'd run out of excuses. Arriving home was a real downer. The temptation to start drinking again was huge. Until Sarah whipped out a folded brown envelope from her pocket and stuffed it into my hand. I recognized the handwriting at once.
	***Callum** enters as she reads.*
Callum	Dear Sephy, I know it's been a long time since we met and you probably don't remember me anymore. But if you do, please could we meet tonight around nine o'clock at our special place. It's very important. But I'll understand if you can't make it.

Two, almost three years is a long time. A lifetime. Callum.

Sephy ponders over whether she should go as we start to hear the sound of the waves.

SCENE 19

*The beach. Night. **Sephy** looks at her watch. **Callum** appears and sneaks up behind her.*

Callum	Surprise!
Sephy	There you are. You made me jump!

Silence.

What's wrong?

Callum suddenly kisses Sephy. Morgan, Pete and Jude approach behind Sephy. Their faces are masked. Callum stops kissing Sephy.

Callum	I'm sorry.

Sephy turns. She tries to escape.

Jude	Over here, Pete.
Pete	Morgan!

She runs into the sea. The noughts follow with torches. They grab her. There is a struggle in the water, with people being pushed above and below the water. Callum joins in. They try to grab Sephy but she breaks free. After a while, Jude grabs Sephy. She hits Jude.

Jude	Bloody dagger bitch.

Jude punches Sephy in the stomach.

That's for my sister.

Sephy is winded. One of the other noughts grabs her and they start dragging her out of the water. One of the noughts takes a hood out of his pocket. They cover her. She passes out.

Hideaway.

Callum   We'd succeeded. We had Sephy. NO! Not Sephy... just a Cross – who deserved everything she got, who'd get us everything we needed. We bundled her into the boot of the car. And now we were in the middle of nowhere. Where no-one would ever find her. Weren't we clever?

Jude   I didn't think you had it in you, little brother.

Callum grabs Jude.

Callum   Don't you ever doubt my loyalty again. D'you understand me?

Morgan steps forward but Pete stops him.

D'you understand?

Jude   So the mouse can roar, can he?

Callum tightens his grip.

Cool it, brother. Peace.

Callum lets him go.

Pete   What's our next move?

Morgan   I dunno.

Jude   We deliver the ransom note with proof we have her to the girl's father.

Callum   What proof?

Jude   What would you suggest, little brother?

Callum   I'll cut off some of her hair. And film her holding today's paper.

Pete   Maybe we need something more convincing than her hair.

Callum   Something of hers that's bloodstained might be more effective.

Jude	Good idea. What would you suggest?
Morgan	Her ear!
Callum	Leave it to me. I'll sort it out.
	*Everyone stares at **Callum**.*
	What are you lot staring at?

● ●

SCENE 21

	*Sephy's cell. **Callum** holds scissors and a camcorder. He removes **Sephy's** hood. He goes to cut a lock of her hair. Their eyes meet. **Jude** and **Leila** stand behind **Callum**.*
Callum	I want you to hold this newspaper.
Sephy	Why?
Jude	I need to film you holding today's paper.
	*Sephy notices **Jude** for the first time.*
Sephy	Jude! Might have known you were behind this.
Callum	It wasn't just him.
Sephy	Whatever. I'm not going to help you.
	*Callum goes to cut her hair again. **Jude** holds her down.*
Jude	Hold that paper or we'll break your arms.
Callum	[*To **Jude***] I don't need you standing over me, supervising.
Jude	Not supervising. Just observing.
Callum	Hold the newspaper, Sephy.
	*Callum holds the paper out. **Sephy** takes it. **Leila**, a fellow nought kidnapper enters.*
Leila	I've come to see the daughter of the famous Kamal Hadley.
Callum	I don't need an audience, thanks.

Leila	Let's see the silver spoon then.
Callum	Leila!
Leila	I bet you've never had more to worry about in your life than chipping the odd fingernail.
Jude	Leila, go and guard the front. Morgan, you go with her.
Leila	*[To Callum]* Later, sweetie.
	Leila kisses Callum and leaves with Morgan.
Sephy	Is that your girlfriend?
	Callum hands Sephy a sheet of paper.
Callum	I want you to read out that message for your father.
	Callum points the camcorder at her. She scrunches the paper up and throws it away.
Sephy	*[To the camera]* Dad, don't give them a penny.
	Jude rushes over to her and grabs her.
Jude	You're not in control in here. We are. And you will do as you're told or you won't leave this place alive. Do you understand?
	Jude drops her.
	You won't get away with your crap around here. We're not your servants anymore.
Callum	I'll handle this.
	Jude goes to exit. He turns back.
Jude	Make sure she does as she's told.
	Jude goes out. Callum picks up the paper and starts smoothing it.
Sephy	I understand why you feel you have to do something. I really do. But this isn't the way.
	Pause.

	Callum, listen to me. At Chivers I became involved in protests and debates and sit-ins. If you try to change the world using violence, you'll just swap one form of injustice for –
Callum	I don't want your ruddy advice thank you. I'm sick of your charity and your handouts. You're just like all the others. You think we noughts can't do a damned thing unless you Crosses are there to help or supervise.
Sephy	Don't hate me for wanting to make a difference. I genuinely –
Callum	Shut up! Hold up the newspaper and read the words on this.

Callum hands her the newspaper.

Read it.

Sephy	Callum, please.
Callum	READ IT!

She reads from the paper. Callum films her.

Sephy	Dad, I've been kidnapped and the kidnappers say you'll never see me again unless you do exactly as you're told. Your instructions will be in the envelope along with this tape. You have twenty-four hours to follow their demands to the letter. If you don't, I'll be killed.

Sephy is crying. Callum zooms in. She wipes her eyes. He finishes filming. He takes out the scissors.

Callum	Now, take your top off.
Sephy	Pardon?
Callum	You heard me.
Sephy	No way.
Callum	Take off your top or I'll do it for you.

She starts taking her top off. He turns away.

Sephy	Are you going to kill me, Callum?
Callum	Just be quiet.

Sephy	Didn't that night mean anything to you?
	Pause.
	It wasn't me who killed your father, Callum. I wanted him to live as much as you did.
Callum	You and your kind killed him.
Sephy	So now you're going to kill me. But not you personally, I bet. That's not your style is it?
Callum	You wouldn't be the first dagger I've killed. Not by a long shot.
Sephy	And I'd be easy to kill, wouldn't I? 'Cause I don't count. I'm nothing. A black dagger bitch. Just like you're a white blanker bastard.
	Jude watches as Callum grabs Sephy and cuts her finger. He wipes the blood on her top.
Callum	That'll prove we mean business.
Sephy	Now your brother really will be impressed.
	Sephy puts her finger in her mouth. Callum takes his jacket off and puts it on her shoulders. She shrugs it off.

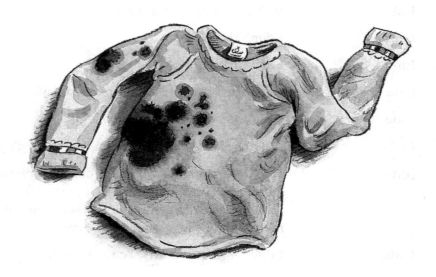

Callum	Suit yourself.
	Callum goes to leave.
Sephy	When you all decide you don't need me any more. I want *you* to do it.
	Callum exits.

●●

SCENE 22

	The hideaway.
Callum	We sent off the tape with Sephy's top. The next day, we gathered round the TV to watch the evening news.
	*Jude clicks the TV on with the remote. **Callum, Jude, Leila, Pete** and **Morgan** watch the TV. Enter **Kamal** and reporters.*
Kamal	I am here to announce that I shall be temporarily withdrawing from public office for personal family reasons. I don't wish to say anything further at this time.
	*Jude clicks the TV off. **Kamal** exits.*
Morgan	Bloodsucking bastard.
Jude	We've got him over a barrel.
Pete	I don't trust him.
Jude	I don't trust any of them.
Pete	What's the plan for the telephone relay?
Jude	Leila should stay here with the girl.
Leila	What, because I'm the girly? I've trained all year for this.
Jude	Pete, Morgan and I will make our relay phone calls from three different locations around town to stop them tracing the calls. Callum will drop off the second set of instructions, pick up our money and head straight back here.
Leila	I think it's better if I make the pick up.

Pete	Good idea. That's always the most dangerous part and, as a girl, she's more likely to go unnoticed.
Callum	Then I'll go in your place and make one of the phone calls.
Jude	No. Of all of us, you're the one Hadley knows the best. We can't take any chances of him recognizing your voice.
Pete	Good thinking.
Callum	I'm not staying here. I'm not a ruddy babysitter.
Jude	You don't have a choice.
Callum	I'm not staying here.
Jude	You're staying behind and that's final. Let's go. And remember Sephy Hadley won't see her dad again til five LM members are released.
	They all get ready to leave.
	If the police or anyone suspicious arrives, you shoot the girl first and ask questions afterwards. Get it?
Callum	Got it.
Pete	Good.
Jude	We're counting on you.
	Leila kisses Callum.
Leila	Stay true to the struggle, comrade.
	They leave Callum on his own.

● ●

SCENE 23

*The cell. **Sephy** lies on her bed. She is rubbing her stomach, clearly still in pain.*

Callum	You should eat something.
Sephy	I'm not hungry.

Callum	I'll leave it here.
	He puts the bowl down on the floor.
Sephy	The voices through the wall have stopped. Have they left you on your own?
Callum	Sephy, even if you hate me now, you're still a part of me. We share a history. No-one can ever take that away.
Sephy	Then let me go.
Callum	I can't.
Sephy	Of course you can. It's up to you. Not Jude. You.
Callum	I'm going now, Sephy.
Sephy	There's no-one else here. You could escape too. I won't tell anyone you were involved. I swear.
Callum	I can't do it, Sephy. No.
Sephy	So much for our history.
	Pause.
Callum	I'll be back in a couple of hours.
Sephy	I need some painkillers. My stomach hurts. The punch.
	Pause.
	Callum *moves towards her. He tries to rub her stomach. She pulls away.*
Callum	I thought we were going to go away together. I guess you went off the idea.
Sephy	Didn't you get my letter?
Callum	What letter?
	Sephy *is crying.*
Sephy	Ignore me. Just go away, please.
Callum	Do you hate me?

Pause.

Do you?

Sephy	*[Aside]* Before I could make a sound, his lips were on mine and I could see nothing but his face, his eyes.
Callum	*[Aside]* I'd daydreamed so many times of doing this. This was something that was never, ever going to happen.
Sephy	*[Aside]* But now the world had turned upside down and Callum was kissing me.
Callum	*[Aside]* This wasn't real. None of it was real. It couldn't be. It was forbidden. Against the law. Against nature.
Sephy	*[Aside]* I was dreaming again. Lost in my world where there were no noughts and Crosses. Just me and Callum, as Callum and I should be.
Callum	*[Aside]* Perhaps if we could just love long enough and hard enough and deep enough, then the world outside would never, ever hurt us again.
Sephy	Callum!
Callum	Shh! I won't hurt you. I'd never hurt you.
Sephy	*[Aside]* His breath was hot and made my insides melt.
Callum	I love you.
Sephy	*[Aside]* I pulled him closer to me, wrapping my arms around him.
Both	*[Aside]* And then, it was as if we'd both caught fire.
Callum	*[Aside]* Sort of like spontaneous combustion.
Sephy	*[Aside]* And we were burning up.
Callum	I love you.
Sephy	*[Aside]* I could hardly hear him over the blood roaring in my ears. Every caress, every stroke robbed me of my breath and burnt through my skin.

Callum	*[Aside]* She unbuttoned my shirt.
Sephy	*[Aside]* He unfastened my bra.
Callum	*[Aside]* She unzipped my trousers.
Both	*[Aside]* We were both naked.
Callum	*[Aside]* And I was shaking. But not from the cold.
Both	*[Aside]* We both knelt on the bed facing each other.
Sephy	*[Aside]* Callum's gaze moved down over my body.
Callum	*[Aside]* I reached out and touched her face.
Sephy	*[Aside]* He ran his hands over my lips and my nose and forehead.
Callum	*[Aside]* I laid her down gently.
Sephy	*[Aside]* His hands and lips exploring my body.
Both	*[Aside]* We were going to make this time last for ever.
Sephy	*[Aside]* I let myself drift away, following wherever Callum led. Beside him all the way as he led me across the frontier into a new real, unreal world.
Both	*[Aside]* Not quite heaven. Not quite hell.

Callum and Sephy sit on the mattress. Sephy is crying. Callum tries to put his arm around her. She pulls away and puts on her sweater. Jude and Morgan enter.

Callum	What's happened?
Jude	You tell us.
Callum	Where's Leila?
Morgan	Arrested.
Callum	What? Where's Pete?
Jude	Dead.
Callum	What?

Jude	They had undercover police everywhere. They must have been monitoring every phone box in town. We were lucky to escape in one piece. I'd thought we could take the girl and move out of here to somewhere safer…
Callum	I'll pack up our equipment.
Jude	I don't think so. Morgan, you do it.

Morgan goes out. Jude switches the light on. Sephy weeps.

You stupid, stupid berk. We're finished.

Jude grabs Callum and hits him during the next lines.

We could have got what we wanted and let her go. They'd never have found us. But not now. Why d'you have to rape her? I'm not going to be the one to get rid of her. You'll have to do it. You stupid, stupid…

Callum punches Jude in the face and Jude falls to the ground.

Callum	Don't you ever hit me again as long as you live.

Jude gets up and attacks Callum. They fight. While they fight, Sephy rushes to the door.

Jude	Stop her! Get her! Morgan!

Sephy has gone. They follow her.

• •

SCENE 24

The forest.

The company create the forest. Sephy weaves around the trees. Callum, Jude and Morgan follow with torches. Sephy hides behind a tree.

Morgan	Over there!
Jude	Persephone!

Pause.

I know you can hear me. We're kilometres away from anywhere here. It's no good trying to run.

Pause.

You'll wander around this forest for days without seeing another soul. There's no food. No water. Come out now and we won't harm you. We promise.

Pause.

If you don't show yourself and we find you...

Jude *signals to the others and they separate off.*

[Wandering off] Sephy, I know you're here somewhere.

Sephy *is close to **Callum**. She appears from behind a tree. **Callum** spots her. He approaches her from behind and grabs her. He puts his hand over her mouth.*

Callum	Shh. It's me.
Morgan	*[Calling]* What was that?
Callum	It's only me. I tripped.
Morgan	I'll go towards the road.
Callum	What's that over there? I think it's her. She must be trying to double back on us. Heading for the cabin.
Jude	Where? Morgan, over here.

Morgan *and **Jude** head off. **Sephy** and **Callum** are alone.*

Callum	Do you see Orion's Belt?

Sephy *nods.*

Always keep it immediately behind you. When you reach the road, turn left on to it and keep going.

Sephy	Callum...
Callum	Quickly, Sephy.
Sephy	Thank you.

They kiss.

Callum   Now go.

Sephy leaves.

• •

SCENE 25

*Outside a private hospital. **Kamal Hadley** enters with his **PR** surrounded by **reporters**. He reads from a sheet of paper.*

Kamal   I... I will make a short statement and... that's it. *[he reads]* My daughter is still unconscious after being found this morning. Her doctors describe her condition as critical but stable. The police are present and will interview her as soon as she regains consciousness. Acting on information received, we captured one of the kidnappers and another opened fire on the police and was killed as a result. No ransom was paid. That's all I'd like to say at this moment.

*He goes to exit, trailed by **journalists** including **the reporter**.*

Reporter   How's your wife bearing up?

Journalist 1   Why did you wait till this morning to reveal that your daughter had been kidnapped?

Journalist 2   What are the extent of Persephone's injuries?

• •

SCENE 26

The beach.

Callum   All the way down to the coast, I phoned Sephy's house using our signal from years ago. I had no idea if she was at the house or even if she heard my signals but I wasn't going to let that stop me. I had to see her. I had to know if the rumours in the press over the last few weeks were true.

*The sound of waves. **Sephy** enters.*

Sephy   You shouldn't have come here. It isn't safe.

Callum	I didn't have a choice.
Sephy	Where are you living?
Callum	Around and about.
Sephy	I thought I'd never see you again.
Callum	Sephy, can I ask you something?
Sephy	OK.
Callum	Why did you cry that night?

Pause.

Did I hurt you? If I did, I'm sorry. I…

Sephy	You know you didn't.
Callum	Then why?
Sephy	When we made love, I knew for sure that I loved you. That I always have and that I always will. But I also realized what you'd been trying to tell me all these years. You're a nought and I'm a Cross and there's no way we could ever be together. Even if we'd gone away, we would've lasted a year, maybe two. But sooner or later, other people would've found a way to wedge us apart. That's what made me cry.
Callum	I understand.

Pause.

You know why I'm here.

Sephy	Yes.
Callum	Well?
Sephy	Minerva guessed before I did.
Callum	Are you going to keep it?
Sephy	Father's trying every trick in the book to stop me.
Callum	But he's not succeeding.
Sephy	Not yet. I don't know. It's difficult.

Pause.

If I do have it and it's a boy, I'm going to call him Ryan after your dad.

Callum	If it's a girl, call her Rose. To remind you of the rose garden where we used to play when we were kids.
Sephy	What about Calluma? Callumetta. Callie. That's good. Callie.
Callum	I prefer Rose.

Pause.

Sephy	When you said… When you said you loved me that night, did you mean it? I don't mind if you didn't. Well I do, but. I mean…
Callum	Let's get out of here. Let's go away. We can be together, even if it's just for a little while, we could…

*Suddenly they're surrounded by **police** holding torches.*

Policeman	Put your hands in the air, McGregor, or we'll shoot.

***Callum** does so. He turns to **Sephy** as the police pull her away.*

Callum	*[To Sephy]* Tell me you didn't know this was going to happen.

● ●

SCENE 27

***Callum's** prison cell.*

Callum	What time is it, Jack?
Jack	Ten to.
Callum	Time for a quick game of rummy?
Jack	Callum…

***Callum** puts down the cards.*

Pause.

Callum	Do you ever wonder what it would be like if our positions were reversed? If we whites were in charge instead of you Crosses?

113

Jack	Can't say I have.
Callum	I used to think about it a lot. How different the world would be.
Jack	People are people. Doesn't matter who's in charge.
Callum	You think so?

Jack shrugs.

Callum	You don't believe that things get better? That they have to one day, some day?
Jack	Your girl, Persephone Hadley, tried to get in here to see you – and more than once as well. But orders came from way above the governor's head that you were to have no visitors whatsoever under any circumstances.

Pause.

Callum	Jack, can I ask you a favour?
Jack	Just name it.
Callum	It might get you into trouble.
Jack	My dull life could do with a bit of sprucing up.
Callum	Could you find a way to deliver this letter to Sephy?

Callum takes an envelope out of his pocket.

Jack	Persephone Hadley?
Callum	That's right.
Jack	Sure thing.

Callum gives Jack the envelope.

Callum	You have to personally put it in her hand. Promise?
Jack	I promise.

Pause.

Callum	What's the time, Jack?

Jack	Five to.

There is the sound of a key in the cell door. Jack hides the letter. In walks Kamal and the prison governor.

Kamal	I'm sure you can guess why I'm here.

Callum doesn't answer.

I'm here to offer you a deal. It's not too late for me to overturn the sentence. If you do what I say, I'll make sure you don't hang. You'll be sentenced to life and I'll guarantee you only serve eight to ten years. You'll come out of prison with your whole life ahead of you.

Callum	And what exactly do I have to do for this… largesse?
Kamal	Sign this.
Callum	What does it say?
Kamal	It states that you raped my daughter and that you want nothing to do with her unborn child.
Callum	Sephy knows that's not true.
Kamal	If you tell her you don't want to be a father to the child, she'll terminate the pregnancy. Then we can all get on with our lives.
Callum	Is it just the thought of Sephy and I having a child together that you can't stand, or is it mixed-race children in general?
Governor	I need to open the public gallery, Sir.
Kamal	Are you going to save your life or the child's?

Callum tears up the confession. Kamal leaves the cell.

Have it your way.

Governor	Do you have a last request?
Callum	Just get it over with.
Governor	Do you want a priest?

Callum shakes his head. Governor nods at Jack and exits.

Jack	Put your hands behind your back, Callum.
	*Jack handcuffs **Callum**.*
	Not long now.
	*They walk down a corridor. **Nought prisoners** reach out to **Callum**.*
Prisoner 1	Good luck, Cal.
Prisoner 2	Spit in their eye, Callum.
Prisoner 3	Good luck.
	*Jack shakes **Callum's** hand.*

● ●

SCENE 28

*Execution chamber. There is a noose and a platform. A large crowd of spectators watches. **Minerva** has her arm around **Sephy**. **Kamal** and **Jasmine** are also there. **Jack** puts the hood over **Callum's** head. Blackout. The prison clock chimes one.*

Sephy	I love you, Callum.
	Two.
	I love you and our child will love you too.
	Three.
	I love you, Callum. I'll always love you.
	Four.
Callum	I love you too, Sephy.
	Five.
Sephy	I love you, Callum.
	Six.
Callum	I love –
	*Blackout. We hear the trapdoor give way and the sound of **Callum's** body swinging. Out of the darkness, we hear **the reporter.***
Reporter	And last night at midnight Deputy Prime Minister Kamal Hadley's daughter, Persephone, gave birth to a girl. Miss Hadley has issued a statement that her daughter, named Callie Rose, will be taking her father's name of McGregor. The Deputy Prime Minister was unavailable for comment.

• •

SCENE 29

The beach.

***Sephy** is sitting on the sand, holding the baby, Callie Rose. She comforts her daughter. She looks out to sea. Lights fade.*

Activities

ACTIVITIES

NOUGHTS AND CROSSES

Framework Substrand	Activities						
	1	2	3	4	5	6	7
1.1 Developing active listening skills and strategies			√				√
1.2 Understanding and responding to what speakers say in formal and informal contexts		√	√			√	√
2.1 Developing and adapting speaking skills and strategies in formal and informal contexts							√
2.2 Using and adapting the conventions and forms of spoken texts			√				√
3.1 Developing and adapting discussion skills and strategies in formal and informal contexts	√	√	√		√	√	√
3.2 Taking roles in group discussion	√		√				√
4.1 Using different dramatic approaches to explore ideas, texts and issues	√	√				√	√
4.2 Developing, adapting and responding to dramatic techniques, conventions and styles	√		√		√	√	
5.1 Developing and adapting active reading skills and strategies	√	√	√	√	√	√	√
5.2 Understanding and responding to ideas, viewpoints, themes and purposes in texts	√		√		√	√	
5.3 Reading and engaging with a wide and varied range of texts							
6.1 Relating texts to the social, historical and cultural contexts in which they were written				√			
6.2 Analysing how writers' use of linguistic and literary features shapes and influences writing					√	√	
6.3 Analysing writers' use of organization, structure, layout and presentation		√			√	√	
7.1 Generating ideas, planning and drafting		√	√				√
7.2 Using and adapting the conventions and forms of texts on paper and screen				√			√
8.1 Developing viewpoint, voice and ideas			√	√	√		
8.2 Varying sentences and punctuation for clarity and effect				√			
8.3 Improving vocabulary for precision and impact				√			√
8.4 Developing varied linguistic and literary techniques				√			√
8.5 Structuring, organizing and presenting texts in a variety of forms on paper and on screen				√			√
8.6 Developing and using editing and proofreading skills on paper and on screen				√			√
9.1 Using the conventions of standard English				√			√
9.2 Using grammar accurately and appropriately				√			√
9.3 Reviewing spelling and increasing knowledge of word derivations, patterns and families				√			√
10.1 Exploring language variation and development according to time, place, culture, society and technology							
10.2 Commenting on language use							

Dramatic moments

The plot of *Noughts and Crosses* moves very quickly over a period of several years. There are many points in the play where characters experience danger, violence, conflict or extreme emotions. These dramatic moments not only drive the plot of the play forward, but can also have a significant impact on the audience, causing them to experience surprise, tension, excitement, shock or sadness.

IDENTIFYING DRAMATIC MOMENTS

Together with a partner, make a list of some of the dramatic moments in the play. It might begin like this:

> – The protest at Heathcroft High School
>
> – Sephy is beaten up by three Cross girls
>
> – Lynette's suicide

TABLEAUX

Now working in small groups, go through the lists you have compiled and choose four key moments in the play. You will be creating tableaux – still images that are like a snapshot of the scene.

- Decide as a group on the exact point at which you will freeze the action in each scene.
- Choose one member of the group to be a director. He or she will need to think carefully about where and how each character should be positioned.
- Allocate parts to each group member. Some may need to act as crowd members or passers-by in scenes where only one or two main characters are present.

- Consider what your character is thinking and feeling at the moment of the 'snapshot'. Try to convey this using your body language and facial expression.

After the tableaux are arranged, the director can take on the role of narrator, commenting on the action and providing a link between scenes.

Perform your tableaux, complete with narration, for the class. Have you all chosen similar dramatic moments?

Assessment

- **Peer assessment**. After each tableaux performance, students in the audience point out why they thought the scenes were effective and how they could be improved. Which four tableaux best summed up the plot of *Noughts and Crosses*?
- **Self-assessment**. Think about your own performance. How well did you portray your character's thoughts and feelings: very well, quite well, or could you have done more? In the case of the director, how well did you use the space available? Did your narration reflect the action effectively?

Staging the play

· ·

DOUBLING ROLES

In his directions on page 8, Dominic Cooke suggests that apart from the main characters and their families, all parts should be doubled. This means that actors are able to act in more than one role.

You are going to create a table showing which characters appear in which scene, to make it easier for actors playing more than one part. Your table should look like this:

Scene	Location	Characters	Production notes
1.1	The beach	Sephy Callum	
1.2	Callum's house	Callum Meggie Ryan Lynette Jude	

Complete the table, leaving the final column blank.

What problems might there be with doubling parts in a play like *Noughts and Crosses*, where half the roles are played by white actors, and half the roles by black actors? How could you solve this problem?

In the 2007 RSC production, the police wore blacked out helmets to hide the fact that some of the actors playing them were white (only Crosses could be policemen in the story).

Look again at the directions on page 7:

> Scenes should flow into one another with no gaps. No blackouts except where stated. There should be a minimum of props and clutter.

In small groups, discuss how you could indicate the different locations in the play without using set changes. Think about:

● Lighting
● Sound
● Use of space (for example, different levels)
● Basic props (remember, these should be kept to a minimum)

Once you have decided how to do this, add relevant notes to your table.

Assessment

● **Peer assessment**. Swap your table with another group. Ask them to consider your staging ideas and suggest one way in which these could be improved.
● **Self assessment**. Consider your contribution to the group activity. See if you can answer yes to both of the following questions:
   ● Did you listen to other students' viewpoints?
   ● Did you put your own ideas forward?

Sephy and Callum

In *Noughts and Crosses,* we meet two characters who have to make big decisions about their lives and what they believe. Sephy and Callum have had very different upbringings: Sephy has led a privileged life while Callum has struggled to make his way in the world. However, they also have things in common: their feelings for one another, as well as their views on equality between noughts and Crosses.

CHARACTER PROFILE

In small groups, decide whether you will be looking at the character of Sephy or Callum. Choose one member of your group to make notes on your discussion. Skim through the text together, taking note of what your chosen character says and does. Remember to look not only at what a character says and does, but also at how other characters describe them and how they react to them.

Decide as a group what the most important things about your character are and note them down in the form of a mind map, such as the one shown here.

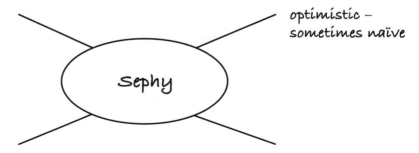

optimistic –
sometimes naïve

Sephy

Assessment

Peer assessment. Swap your character profile with another group who are looking at the other character. Ask them to note down any points they think are missing.

Choose one person in the group to role-play your character in a hot seating activity. Place two chairs at the front of the class and have one 'Sephy' and one 'Callum' sit in each of them (students can rotate as the exercise progresses to give each group a chance). The class ask the two characters questions about how they feel and why they behave in a particular way, and they answer in role, referring back to the play as often as possible.

You could ask the characters to imagine they are answering from their perspective at a particular point in the play, such as when Sephy goes to boarding school and Callum joins the Liberation Militia.

Assessment

- **Self assessment.** How well do you think you performed in the hot seating activity (either as a questioner or a performer)? Rate yourself from 1–3 (three being the highest).
- **Peer assessment.** As a group, decide which performance in role was most convincing.

Segregation

Although *Noughts and Crosses* is a work of fiction, some of the incidents in it closely reflect real events. For example, the Dundale shopping centre bombing is similar to an IRA bombing at the Arndale centre in Manchester in 1996. Act 1 Scene 3 also has many echoes of events that took place in Little Rock, Arkansas in 1957.

THE LITTLE ROCK NINE

Up until the 1950s, many areas of the USA still had separate schools for black and white children. In 1954, the Supreme Court declared this to be unconstitutional. However, there was a lot of resistance to racial integration in the Southern states. On 4 September 1957, a crisis developed at one school in Little Rock when nine black students tried to enter the school for the first time. They were prevented from doing so by the Governor, who sent soldiers from the Arkansas National Guard to block the entrance, and were surrounded by hostile crowds. Ultimately, President Dwight Eisenhower had to send federal troops to escort the students into the school.

One of the Nine, Elizabeth Eckford, wrote the following account of what happened:

I stood looking at the school – it looked so big! Just then the guards let some white students go through.

The crowd was quiet. I guess they were waiting to see what was going to happen. When I was able to steady my knees, I walked up to the guard who had let the white students in. He didn't move. When I tried to squeeze past him, he raised his bayonet and then the other guards closed in and they raised their bayonets.

They glared at me with a mean look and I was very

frightened and didn't know what to do. I turned around and the crowd came toward me.

They moved closer and closer. Somebody started yelling, "Lynch her! Lynch her!"

I tried to see a friendly face somewhere in the mob – someone who maybe would help. I looked into the face of an old woman and it seemed a kind face, but when I looked at her again, she spat on me.

- Do some more research on the Little Rock Nine and the American civil rights movement in general. Make a note of dates, key names and events.
- Write a short, clear summary of one of these events. Remember to write in standard English and to include facts rather than opinions.

Assessment

Peer assessment. Swap your summary with another student. Can they make it shorter without leaving out any important information?

• •

DIARY EXTRACT

Look at Act 1 Scene 3 (page 19). In this scene, Callum and two other noughts face an angry mob on their first day at Heathcroft School. Read through the scene and try to imagine how they feel.

- Now write a short extract from the perspective of one of these three characters (Callum, Shania or Colin).
- Use the first person when talking about yourself, and the third person when talking about others.
- Recount what has happened using the past tense.
- Talk about your thoughts and feelings using the present tense.
- Predict what might happen in the coming days or weeks using the future tense.

Assessment

- **Self assessment**. Check your diary entry against the list above. Give yourself a thumbs up 👍 or a thumbs down 👎 for each item.
- **Peer assessment**. Swap your diary entry with another student. Ask them to point out two things they liked about your piece, and one thing they feel could be improved. You may like to redraft your work, taking their suggestions into account.

Narrative viewpoint

Malorie Blackman wrote *Noughts and Crosses* from two
different perspectives: half of the story is told by Sephy, and
the other half by Callum. Both narrators speak in the first
person. She has said that she used this technique because she
wanted the society in her book to be viewed from two different
points of view to show how our perspectives colour our
thinking.

TWO PERSPECTIVES

Dominic Cooke has used a similar technique in the play.
Throughout the performance, Sephy and Callum speak
directly to the audience. What is the effect of including these
monologues?

Write a list of similarities and differences between Sephy's and
Callum's narratives in the play. How are their 'voices' different?
Think about:
- whether their voices change as the play progresses
- how they talk about each other
- how they talk about their own and each other's families
- their outlooks on life, and how each deals with problems.

Assessment

- **Peer assessment**. Swap your list with a partner. Discuss
  where there are differences between them.

OTHER CHARACTERS

All the other characters in *Noughts and Crosses* also have
unique viewpoints. Although they don't speak to the audience
in the way that Sephy and Callum do, we can understand a lot
about them from what they say to one another.

Read the following quotations. They are all taken from the playscript and spoken by major characters other than Sephy and Callum. Working in pairs, decide who says what. You should focus on matching the ideas and attitudes expressed with who is most likely to say them, rather than looking the speeches up in your playscript.

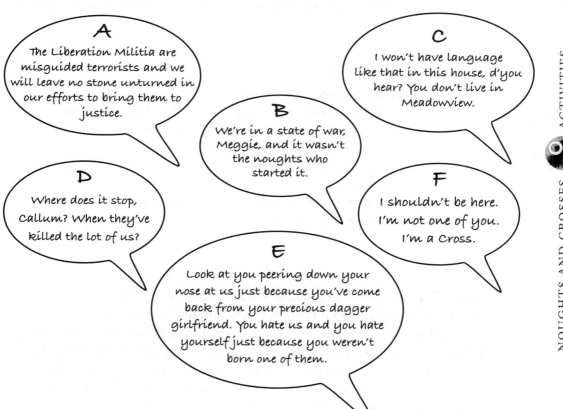

A
The Liberation Militia are misguided terrorists and we will leave no stone unturned in our efforts to bring them to justice.

B
We're in a state of war, Meggie, and it wasn't the noughts who started it.

C
I won't have language like that in this house, d'you hear? You don't live in Meadowview.

D
Where does it stop, Callum? When they've killed the lot of us?

E
Look at you peering down your nose at us just because you've come back from your precious dagger girlfriend. You hate us and you hate yourself just because you weren't born one of them.

F
I shouldn't be here. I'm not one of you. I'm a Cross.

Assessment

- **Peer assessment.** Join up with one or two other pairs and discuss your answers. Where you disagree, give clear reasons why you think a quote comes from a particular character.
- **Teacher assessment.** Ask your teacher to check whether your answers are correct, using the playscript as a reference.

From novel to playscript

The *Noughts and Crosses* playscript is adapted from the novel by Malorie Blackman. It would, of course, be impossible to include everything from the novel in the play, so the playwright has had to make decisions about what he will leave in and what he will take out.

COMPARING NOVEL AND PLAY

Read the following extract from the novel version of *Noughts and Crosses* and then compare it to Act 2 Scene 19 on page 98. As you read both of these texts, consider:

- what has and has not been included
- how the description in the novel has been conveyed in the playscript
- how the dialogue differs or is similar
- how character is conveyed.

I glanced at my watch, wondering where Callum had got to. I turned, almost as if thinking about Callum would conjure him up. I gasped. Callum was standing right behind me, his appearance so sudden that he might've been a ghost, able to appear and disappear at will. And he looked so different. He'd shot up like a beanstalk. He was lean now, rather than skinny. He'd definitely sprouted muscles! And his dark cords and leather jacket made him look... mysterious somehow. His hair was longer too, almost shoulder-length. It suited him. Everything about him seemed different. Callum the boy had disappeared and in his place... I smiled, chiding myself. It was as if I'd expected time to stand still for him. I'm glad it hadn't though! Had I changed as much? I guess I must've.

'Good sneaking!' I congratulated him with a wry smile.

Slipping on my sandals, I stepped forward, my arms outstretched for a hug. I expected a similar jovial reply in greeting, but he didn't even smile.

And even in this light, I could tell something was wrong. My arms dropped to my sides.

'Callum?'

Callum stepped forward and kissed me. A brief, icy-cold kiss on the lips. He stepped away from me, his eyes filled with regret. And then I saw them behind him. Four of them. Four noughts. Walking towards us. Towards me. A quick glance at Callum. Shock on my face. Confirmation, resignation on his. And I didn't wait to see any more. I turned and ran. Ran along the shore. Away from them. Away from Callum. Ran for my life. I could hear them yelling behind me. Not the words. I didn't try to decipher the words.

Run, Sephy. Don't stop…

PERFORMANCE

Working in groups, discuss how a reading of the novel might affect a performance of the scene and the way that both action and character are portrayed.

Rehearse a performance of the scene, using the ideas you have explored.

Assessment

- **Peer assessment**. Perform your scene for another group. When you have finished, perform it again, but this time invite them to suggest ways of changing the performance as you go along. They can explore movement and voice, or even swap roles to demonstrate how their suggestions might work.

Breaking news

An interesting aspect to the playscript is the way that news reports are used to deliver information to the characters, often about events that have happened offstage. In each case, the reporter speaks directly to other characters. In real life, of course, television news is delivered to a camera.

REPORTING ON SEPHY'S KIDNAP

Read through Act 2 Scene 26, where Kamal makes a statement about Sephy's rescue to journalists. Working in groups, you are going to use this scene as the basis of a television news report.

1   Appoint a chairperson to ensure everyone in the group has the chance to contribute, as well as someone to make notes of the decisions made.

2   As a group, discuss how to structure your report. You should have:

●   a summary of what has happened (i.e. how Sephy was rescued)

●   an excerpt from Kamal's statement.

You may also like to include:

●   a review of events (Sephy's kidnapping, Kamal's resignation)

●   interviews with police, witnesses, doctors, etc.

●   background information on the kidnappers, the Liberation Militia, etc.

3   Decide who will present the report, and divide up the other roles among the group. Then split up into smaller groups or pairs, and assign each one a portion of the report to write.

4   Bring the group together again and look through the whole report. If necessary, agree on ways to link the different parts of it together.

5   Present your broadcast to the rest of the class.

Assessment

- **Peer assessment**. Ask the class to comment on your performance. What did they think were the strengths of the broadcast, and what needed to be improved?
- **Self-assessment**. Think about how you worked in the group. Give yourself a mark out of three for each of the following (three being the highest):
  - Did you contribute to the group discussion?
  - Did you illustrate and explain your ideas?
  - Did you listen carefully and respond to others' contributions?

Further activities

1   In the play, we never find out what Sephy wrote in her letter asking Callum to run away with her (although the letter does appear in the novel). Try to imagine Sephy's feelings in Act 2 Scene 16 and write your own version of the letter.

2   *Noughts and Crosses* is often compared to William Shakespeare's *Romeo and Juliet*, although Malorie Blackman has said she was not aware of the parallels between the stories until after she had started to write her novel. Find out more about *Romeo and Juliet*, and make a list of the similarities and differences between the plots of the two plays.

3   Although *Noughts and Crosses* is about racism, it is not limited to conflict over colour. It could represent conflict between groups in other contexts and cultures. It is about two people who want to be together, despite their different backgrounds. Sketch out a story about a similar couple who come from different groups or cultures.

4   Tragic stories like *Noughts and Crosses* have been told in many forms, including ballads and epic poems. Write a rap, poem or song telling the story of Sephy and Callum.